The Singing Brakeman

A Jimmie Rodgers Discography

Compiled By
Christian Scott

Every effort has been made by the author and publisher of this book to provide accurate information on the subject matter of this book. Even though the information in this book has been carefully checked and researched, the author and publisher disclaim any responsibility for any errors and or omissions.

No portion of this book may be reproduced in any form or by any means, electronic or mechanical, including recording, photocopying, or by any storage or retrieval system, without the written permission from the author and publisher.

This book is dedicated my wife Eileen, my best friend, the love of my life, a wonderful woman with a beautiful soul and a giving heart.

The Singing Brakeman - A Jimmie Rodgers Discography
Copyright 2015 R. Lees
All Rights Reserved.

This book is in no way endorsed by or associated with any individuals, recording artist(s) / group(s) or companies that are included within this book.

All Pictures and Names Used Remain "Trademark" and "Copyright" of Their Respective Rights Holders.

Acknowledgments

I would like to express my appreciation to all the people who contributed their time, assistance, research and their knowledge throughout the process of creating this reference guide. Their assistance has been indispensable.

Table of Contents

About the Book	5
78 RPM Listing Examples	7
Introduction	8
78 RPM Record Discography:	
Victor Record Label	11
Bluebird Record Label	40
Electradisk Record label	54
Montgomery Ward Record Label	58
Sunrise Record Label	79
Record Photographs	85
Additional Recording Sessions	101
Unissued Tracks Listing	103
45 & 33 RPM Record Discography:	
45 RPM Singles & E.P.	112
33 RPM (Album's / LP's)	116
Foreign Release 45 & 33 RPM	124
Jimmie Rodgers Song Writing Credits	133
Bibliography	141
Performer Index	142
Song Index	144

About The Book

This book is designed to be a reference guide for Jimmie Rodgers' recordings which were recorded by the Victor record company between 1927 - 1933.

This book is organized as follows;

Victor Record Label 78 RPM Listings

> Below each Victor listing you will find additional records that a track was issued on including many foreign issues.

Bluebird Record Label 78 RPM Listings

> Below each Bluebird listing you will find the original Victor record catalogue number that issued that track.

> In the case that Bluebird was the first issue of any track you will find additional records that a track was issued on including many foreign issues.

Electradisk Record Label 78 RPM Listings

> Below each Electradisk listing you will find the original Victor record catalogue number that issued that track.

> In the case that Bluebird was the first issue of any track you will find the Bluebird catalogue record number that issued that track

Montgomery Ward Record Label 78 RPM Listings

> Below each Montgomery Ward listing you will find the original Victor record catalogue number that issued that track.

> In the case that Bluebird was the first issue of any track you will find the Bluebird catalogue record number that issued that track

Sunrise Record Label 78 RPM Listings

> Below each Sunrise listing you will find the original Victor record catalogue number that issued that track.

> In the case that Bluebird was the first issue of any track you will find the Bluebird catalogue record number that issued that track

Additional Recording Sessions (Overdub and Re-Mastering Sessions)

These sessions were undertaken after Jimmie Rodgers' death

Unissued Track Listings

There were many takes of many tracks that were initially unissued these tracks are listed in this section.

- Many of these tracks can now be found on CD.

45 RPM Singles & EP's (Extended Play Records)

This section covers most U.S. pressings with some UK and Australia releases.

LP's (Long Play Albums)

This section covers most U.S. pressings with some UK, Japan and Australia releases.

Jimmie Rodgers Song Writing Credits

This section includes the songs Jimmie Rodgers has written and co-written

Many references have been consulted in order to complete this guide. However, I am sure that errors and omissions are present and I hope that they will be brought to my attention.

78 RPM Listing Examples

Example 1 (If recorded at the same session with same accompaniments)
Record Label & Number
Vocal and instrument accompaniments and personnel
Location and date of recording session
1st Matrix number and track title
2nd Matrix number and track title
VICTOR 20864
    Own, vocal; Own, guitar
    Bristol, Tennessee   August 4, 1927
    39767-4   The Soldier's Sweetheart
    39768-3   Sleep, Baby, Sleep

Example 2 (If recorded on a different date, location, with different personnel etc.)
Record Label & Number
Vocal and instrument accompaniments and personnel
Location and date of recording session
1st Matrix number and track title
Record Label & Number
Vocal and instrument accompaniments
Location and date of recording session
2nd Matrix number and track title
VICTOR 21245
    Own, vocal; Own, guitar
    Camden, New Jersey   November 30, 1927
    40751-2   Ben Dewberry's Final Run
VICTOR 21245
    Own, vocal; Own, guitar; Ellsworth T. Cozzens, banjo
    Camden, New Jersey   February 15, 1928
    41740-1   In The Jailhouse Now

Introduction

Jimmie Rodgers was born James Charles Rodgers on September 8, 1897 in Meridian, Mississippi. By about age 13 Jimmie Rodgers' was very interested in the "entertainment" industry as he had started at least two different traveling road shows and would run off with them. It wasn't long before his father would end up bringing him back home. Soon after that his father had found his son his first legitimate job, working on the railroad as a water boy. It wasn't until a few years later that Jimmie took over his brother Walter's old job as a railroad brakeman on the New Orleans and Northwestern Railroad – his brother Walter moved up to a conductor's position.

It was around 1924 when Jimmie Rodgers contracted Tuberculosis and would temporarily end his railroad career, but he saw this as an opportunity. He once again started a traveling road show which would perform across the southeast. After a severe storm destroyed his traveling show facilities he went back to work in Miami, Florida as a railroad brakeman once again. His illness again caught up with him and he lost his job, from there he relocated to Tucson, Arizona and took a job at the Southern Pacific Railroad as a switchman. Less than a year later he moved back to Meridian with his wife Carrie and daughter Anita, it was now 1927.

On or about April 18, 1927 he arrived in Asheville, North Carolina where he and Otis Kuykendall performed for the first time on Asheville's WWNC radio station. In the early summer Jimmie found a group called the Tenneva Ramblers which included Jack and Claude Grant, Jack Pierce and Claude Sagle which was performing in Tennessee together they decided to go to Ashville's WWNC radio station and were able to secure a weekly time slot to perform as "The Jimmie Rodgers Entertainers".

Sometime in late July 1927, Jimmie Rodgers and the Tenneva Ramblers heard rumors that Ralph Peer was heading to Bristol, Tennessee to hold auditions for any local musicians. Ralph Peer worked for the Victor Talking Machine Company or the Victor Record Label. Jimmie and the Ramblers decided to head out to Bristol and arrived there on August 3. There they auditioned for Ralph Peer in an empty warehouse. After the audition Peer agreed to record the group the following day. Later that night, as the story goes, Jimmie Rodgers and the Tenneva Ramblers Began to discuss how they would be billed on the record, an agreement could not be reached and an argument started. The next morning Jimmie Rodgers was the only one to show up for the recording session with Ralph Peer.

So on August 4, 1927 Jimmie Rodgers had the very first recording session of his career, although he had no accompanying personnel that did not affect the session in the least. The session actually got started about 2:00 and lasted until almost 4:30, two songs were recorded from this session the very first was "The Soldier's Sweetheart" and the second track was "Sleep, Baby, Sleep" both would be issued at a later date. Jimmie would sing and play guitar for both songs and for "Sleep, Baby, Sleep" he would also yodel, this would be his first recorded yodel, this is significant in the fact that Jimmie Rodgers would become one of the best, if not the best yodeler to ever record (in my opinion) and this would show in the vast number of his future recordings.

A Few Things You May Not Know;

It is unclear how many "Takes" were recorded for each song however, "Take 4" was used for "The Soldier's Sweetheart" and "Take 3" was used for "Sleep, Baby, Sleep" on the Victor record 20864. One hundred dollars was what he was paid to record those two tracks on August 4, 1927.

One thing that many people may be unaware of is that Jimmie Rodgers made a film short for Columbia Pictures in October 1929. The film title was "The Singing Brakeman", (I urge anyone who has not seen this to view it on YouTube.)

On July 16, 1930 in Hollywood, California Jimmie Rodgers recorded in 2 Takes "Blue Yodel No. 9" accompanied by Louis Armstrong on trumpet and his wife Lil "Harden" Armstrong on piano ("Harden" was her maiden name).

In August of 1932 Jimmie Rodgers recorded alongside Clayton McMichen, one of the songs they chose to record was McMichen's own "Prohibition Has Done Me Wrong", also accompanying them was Oddie McWinders and Hoyt "Slim" Bryant. There were two known takes of this track of which neither were ever released. McMichen had been under contract with the Columbia Record Label since 1926 and had just ended that relationship about a year earlier in 1931. Columbia claimed the rights to the song that McMichen wrote (at least part of the rights) and would not concede the use of that song to the Victor Record Label. Till this day I have not been able to find any existing recording of Jimmie Rodgers' "Prohibition Has Done Me Wrong" not even on CD. Do the Test Pressings still exist???

The Last Days Of Jimmie Rodgers

Jimmie Rodgers last recording session was in New York City in May of 1933. On May 17 he recorded four tracks by himself, no accompaniments. On May 18 he recorded three more tracks (one of which was not issued on 78 RPM) again he was by himself. His illness was a continuing problem and fatigue would settle in quickly and stay with him most days. He took May 19th off and returned to the recording studio on May 20 there he recorded two more tracks and once again with no accompaniments. He took several more days off and on May 24 he returned to the studio, this time he would be accompanied by John Cali on steel guitar, banjo and guitar along with Tony Colicchio on guitar. Together they recorded three more tracks. Later that same day Jimmie Rodgers would make his very last recording and he would do it alone with no accompaniments just his vocals and his guitar. That very last track that he would record was "Years Ago" the very first "Take" was used and it was issued on Bluebird B-5281. During this last day of recording Jimmie Rodger was said to be so tired and so weak from Tuberculosis that he would rest on a cot between takes.

On May 26, 1933 James Charles "Jimmie" Rodgers died from a pulmonary hemorrhage at the Taft Hotel in New York City, he was 35 years old.

When The Country Music Hall Of Fame was established in 1961 Jimmie Rodgers was one of the first three people to be inducted into the "Hall Of Fame" – the other two were Hank Williams and Fred Rose.

This would be a statement that would resolute until today that Jimmie Rodgers was and is "The Father Of Country Music".

VICTOR Label Releases

The Victor Talking Machine Company or the Victor Record Label was the company that recorded and released all of Jimmie Rodgers tracks from 1927 – 1933, including on their subsidiary and or budget labels

You will find below, each records information, including additional releases on other record labels for that track, matrix number and "Take" number (when known).

Also included below the record information are any foreign listings along with their respective record labels. This listing is not meant to be exhaustive as there were other countries that issued some of these tracks such as South Africa, India and perhaps others that have not been included in this discography.

VICTOR 20864

Own, vocal; Own, guitar

Bristol, Tennessee   August 4, 1927

39767-4   The Soldier's Sweetheart

39768-3   Sleep, Baby, Sleep

Bluebird B-6225 – *"Sleep, Baby, Sleep"* only

Bluebird 33-0513 - *"The Soldiers Sweetheart"* only

Montgomery Ward M-4452

Regal-Zonophone (Australia) G-23197

HMV (Australia) EA-1400

Regal-Zonophone (UK) MR2795 – *"Sleep, Baby, Sleep"* only

Victor (Japan) A1466 – *"Sleep, Baby, Sleep"* only

VICTOR 21142

    Own, vocal, yodel; Own, guitar
    Camden, New Jersey   November 30, 1927
    40753-2   Blue Yodel
    40754-2   Away Out On The Mountain

Bluebird B-5085
Montgomery Ward M-3272
Sunrise S-3172
Victor (Reissue) 21-0042
Regal-Zonophone (UK) T5158
Zonophone (UK) 5158
Regal-Zonophone (Ireland) IZ310
Regal-Zonophone (Australia) EE109 – *"Away Out on the Mountain"* only

VICTOR 21245

    Own, vocal; Own, guitar
    Camden, New Jersey   November 30, 1927
    40751-2   Ben Dewberry's Final Run

VICTOR 21245

    Own, vocal; Own, guitar; Ellsworth T. Cozzens, banjo
    Camden, New Jersey   February 15, 1928
    41740-1   In The Jailhouse Now

Bluebird B-5223 *"In The Jailhouse Now"* only
Bluebird B-5482 *"Ben Dewberry's Final Run"* only
Electradisk 2109 *"In The Jailhouse Now"* only
Sunrise S-3306 *"In The Jailhouse Now"* only
Regal-Zonophone (Australia) G-23117 *"Ben Dewberry's Final Run"* only
Regal-Zonophone (Australia) G-23202 *"In The Jailhouse Now"* only
HMV (Australia) EA-1406 *"In The Jailhouse Now"* only
HMV (Australia) EA-1543 *"Ben Dewberry's Final Run"* only
Regal-Zonophone (Ireland) IZ495 *"Ben Dewberry's Final Run"* only

VICTOR 21291

    Own, vocal, yodel, guitar; Acc. The Three Southerners; Ellsworth T. Cozzens, ukulele

    Camden, New Jersey   February 14, 1928

    41738-1   The Brakeman's Blues (Yodeling The Blues Away)

VICTOR 21291

    Own, vocal, guitar; Acc. Ellsworth T. Cozzens, steel guitar

    Camden, New Jersey   February 15, 1928

    41741-2   Blue Yodel – No. II (My Lovin' Gal Lucille)

Montgomery Ward M-4214

Montgomery Ward M-8121 "Blue Yodel – No. II (My Lovin' Gal Lucille)" only

Victor (Reissue) 21-0044 "The Brakeman's Blues (Yodeling The Blues Away)" only

Victor (Reissue) 21-0181 "Blue Yodel – No. II (My Lovin' Gal Lucille)" only

Regal-Zonophone (Australia) G-23116

HMV (Australia) EA 1542

Regal-Zonophone (Ireland) IZ1004 "The Brakeman's Blues (Yodeling The Blues Away)" only

Regal-Zonophone (UK) MR 3122 "The Brakeman's Blues (Yodeling The Blues Away)" only

VICTOR 21433

    Own, vocal; Own, guitar

    Camden, New Jersey   November 30, 1927

    40752   If Brother Jack Were Here

    (This was the song title at the initial release of this record it is unknown how many records were released with the first title before being changed to "My Mother Was A Lady")

    40752   My Mother Was A Lady

VICTOR 21433

    Own, vocal, yodel; Acc. The Three Southerners; Ellsworth T. Cozzens, steel guitar; Julian R. Ninde, guitar

    Camden, New Jersey   February 14, 1928

    41737-2   Treasures Untold

Bluebird B-5482 *"My Mother Was A Lady"* only

Bluebird B-5838 *"Treasures Untold"* only

Montgomery Ward M-4217 *"Treasures Untold"* only

Montgomery Ward M-4224 *"My Mother Was A Lady"* only

Regal-Zonophone (Australia) G-23193 *"My Mother Was A Lady"* only

Regal-Zonophone / Zonophone (Australia) EE139 *"Treasures Untold"* only

HMV (Australia) EA-1382 *"My Mother Was A Lady"* only

Regal-Zonophone (Ireland) IZ495 *"My Mother Was A Lady"* only

Regal-Zonophone (UK) MR 2241 *"My Mother Was A Lady"* only

VICTOR 21531

    Own, vocal, guitar;

    Camden, New Jersey   February 15, 1928

    41743-2   Blue Yodel No. 3

VICTOR 21531

    Own, vocal, yodel, guitar

    Camden, New Jersey   June 12, 1928

    45099-1   Never No Mo' Blues

Bluebird B-6225 "Never No Mo' Blues" only

Montgomery Ward M-4213 "Blue Yodel No. 3" only

Victor (Reissue) 20-6408 "Never No Mo' Blues" only

Victor (Reissue) 21-0043 "Never No Mo' Blues" only

Victor (Reissue) 21-0177 "Blue Yodel No. 3" only

Regal-Zonophone / Zonophone (Australia) EE109 "Never No Mo' Blues" only

Regal-Zonophone (Ireland) IZ314

Regal-Zonophone (UK) T5247

Zonophone (UK) 5247

VICTOR 21574

    Own, vocal, yodel, ukulele; Acc. The Three Southerners; Ellsworth T. Cozzens, steel guitar, mandolin; Julian R. Ninde, guitar

    Camden, New Jersey   February 14, 1928

    41736-1   Dear Old Sunny South By The Sea

VICTOR 21574

    Own, vocal, yodel, guitar

    Camden, New Jersey   June 12, 1928

    45093-1   My Little Old Home Down In New Orleans

Bluebird B-5609 *"My Little Old Home Down In New Orleans"* only

Bluebird B-6246 *"Dear Old Sunny South By The Sea"* only

Montgomery Ward M-4218 *"My Little Old Home Down In New Orleans"* only

Regal-Zonophone / Zonophone (Australia) EE139 *"My Little Old Home Down In New Orleans"* only

Regal-Zonophone (Australia) G-23188 *"Dear Old Sunny South By The Sea"* only

HMV (Australia) EA 1228 *"Dear Old Sunny South By The Sea"* only

Regal-Zonophone (Ireland) IZ317

Regal-Zonophone (UK) T5341

Zonophone (UK) 5341

Victor (Japan) A1454 *"Dear Old Sunny South By The Sea"* only

VICTOR 21636

    Own, vocal, guitar; Acc. Ellsworth T. Cozzens, steel guitar

    Camden, New Jersey   February 15, 1928

    41742-2   Memphis Yodel

VICTOR 21636

    Own, vocal, guitar;

    Camden, New Jersey   June 12, 1928

    45098-2   Lullaby Yodel

Bluebird B-5337 "Lullaby Yodel" only

Montgomery Ward M-4218 "Lullaby Yodel" only

Montgomery Ward M-4450, M-4725 "Memphis Yodel" only

Sunrise S-3418 "Lullaby Yodel" only
Victor (Reissue) 21-0042 "Memphis Yodel" only
Regal-Zonophone (Australia) G 23114
HMV (Australia) EA 1540
Regal-Zonophone (Ireland) IZ315
Zonophone (UK) 5283
Regal-Zonophone (UK) T5283

VICTOR 21757

Own, vocal, guitar;

Camden, New Jersey	June 12, 1928
45090-1	My Old Pal
45095-1	Daddy And Home

Bluebird B-5991 "Daddy And Home" only
Bluebird B-5609 "My Old Pal" only
Victor (Reissue) 20-6408 "Daddy And Home" only
Victor (Reissue) 21-0043 "Daddy And Home" only
Victor (Reissue) 21-0176 "My Old Pal" only
Regal-Zonophone / Zonophone (Australia) EE150
Regal-Zonophone (Ireland) IZ318
Zonophone (UK) 5356
Regal-Zonophone T5356

VICTOR 22072

Own, vocal, guitar;

New York City	February 23, 1929
49990-2	Blue Yodel No. 5
49992-1	I'm Sorry We Met

Montgomery Ward M-4212 "Blue Yodel No. 5" only
Regal-Zonophone / Zonophone (Australia) EE185
Regal-Zonophone (Ireland) IZ326 "I'm Sorry We Met" only
Regal-Zonophone / Zonophone (UK) T5548 / 5548

VICTOR 22143

    Own, vocal, guitar; Acc. Joe Kaipo, steel guitar; Billy Burkes, guitar; Weldon Burkes, Ukulele

    Dallas, Texas   August 8, 1929

    55307-2   Everybody Does It In Hawaii

VICTOR 22143

    Own, vocal, guitar;

    Dallas, Texas   August 10, 1929

    55333-2   Frankie And Johnny

Bluebird B-5223 " Frankie And Johnny" only

Electradisk 2109 " Frankie And Johnny" only

Montgomery Ward M-4309, M-4721 " Frankie And Johnny" only

Sunrise S-3306 " Frankie And Johnny" only

Victor (Reissue) 21-0044" Frankie And Johnny" only

Regal-Zonophone / Zonophone (Australia) EE189

Regal-Zonophone (Ireland) IZ327

Regal-Zonophone (UK) T5577

Zonophone (UK) 5577

VICTOR 22220

    Own, vocal, guitar; Acc. Joe Kaipo, steel guitar; Billy Burkes, guitar; Weldon Burkes, Ukulele; Bob MacGimsey, whistle

    Dallas, Texas   August 8, 1929

    55308-1   Tuck Away My Lonesome Blues

VICTOR 22220

    Own, vocal, guitar; Acc. Joe Kaipo, steel guitar;

    Dallas, Texas   October 22, 1929

    56455-1   My Rough And Rowdy Ways

Bluebird B-5664 "Tuck Away My Lonesome Blues" only

Montgomery Ward M-4215 "My Rough And Rowdy Ways" only

Montgomery Ward M-5036 "Tuck Away My Lonesome Blues" only

Victor (Reissue) 21-0181

Regal-Zonophone / Zonophone (Australia) EE269

Regal-Zonophone (UK) T5983 "Tuck Away My Lonesome Blues" only

Regal-Zonophone (UK) T6022 "My Rough And Rowdy Ways" only

Zonophone (UK) 5983 "Tuck Away My Lonesome Blues" only

Zonophone (UK) 6022 "My Rough And Rowdy Ways" only

VICTOR 22271

 Own, guitar;

 Dallas, Texas   October 22, 1929

 56453-3   Blue Yodel No. 6

VICTOR 22271

 Own, guitar;

 Dallas, Texas   October 22, 1929

 56454-3   Yodeling Cowboy

Bluebird B-5991 "Yodeling Cowboy" only

Montgomery Ward M_4058, M-4213 "Yodeling Cowboy" only

Montgomery Ward M-4211 "Blue Yodel No. 6" only

Victor (Reissue) 21-0182 "Blue Yodel No. 6" only

Regal-Zonophone (Australia) T5623

Zonophone (Australia) 5623

Regal-Zonophone (Ireland) IZ329

Regal-Zonophone (UK) T5623

Zonophone (UK) 5623

VICTOR 22319

 Acc. Joe Kaipo, steel guitar; Billy Burkes, guitar; Weldon Burkes, ukulele

 Dallas, Texas   October 22, 1929

 56449-3   Whisper Your Mother's Name

VICTOR 22319

 Acc. Joe Kaipo, steel guitar; Billy Burkes, guitar; Weldon Burkes, ukulele

 Atlanta, Georgia   November 28, 1929

 56618-1   A Drunkard's Child

Bluebird B-5057 "Whisper Your Mother's Name" only

Electradisk 1983 "Whisper Your Mother's Name" only

Montgomery Ward M-4207 "Whisper Your Mother's Name" only

Montgomery Ward M-4221 "A Drunkard's Child" only

Sunrise S-3142 "Whisper Your Mother's Name" only

Regal-Zonophone (Australia) G 23193 "Whisper Your Mother's Name" only

Regal-Zonophone (Australia) G 23194 "A Drunkard's Child" only

HMV (Australia) EA 1382 "Whisper Your Mother's Name" only

HMV (Australia) EA 1385 "A Drunkard's Child" only

Regal_Zonophone (Ireland) IZ496 "Whisper Your Mother's Name" only

Regal-Zonophone (UK) MR 2242 "Whisper Your Mother's Name" only

VICTOR 22379

Own, vocal, guitar; Acc. Joe Kaipo, steel guitar; Billy Burkes, guitar; Weldon Burkes, Ukulele; Bob MacGimsey, whistle

Dallas, Texas   August 8, 1929

55309-2   Train Whistle Blues

VICTOR 22379

Own, vocal, guitar; Acc. Joe Kaipo, steel guitar; Billy Burkes, guitar;

Dallas, Texas   August 10, 1929

55332-2   Jimmie's Texas Blues

Montgomery Ward M-4212 "Jimmie's Texas Blues" only

Montgomery Ward M-4223 "Train Whistle Blues" only

Regal-Zonophone (Australia) G23113

HMV (Australia) EA 1539

Regal-Zonophone (UK) T5697

Zonophone (UK) 5697

VICTOR 22421

Own, vocal, vocal effects; Acc. Billy Burkes, guitar;

New Orleans, Louisiana or Atlanta, Georgia (Unclear Where Session Was Recorded)   November 13, 1929

56528-1   Hobo Bill's Last Ride

VICTOR 22421

    Acc. Billy Burkes, guitar;

    Atlanta, Georgia   November 28, 1929

    56619-1   That's Why I'm Blue

Bluebird B-6198 "That's Why I'm Blue" only

Montgomery Ward M-4210 "Hobo Bill's Last Ride" only

Montgomery Ward M-4221 "That's Why I'm Blue" only

Regal-Zonophone / Zonophone (Australia) EE213

Regal-Zonophone (Ireland) IZ333

Regal-Zonophone (Ireland) IZ422 "That's Why I'm Blue" only

Regal-Zonophone (UK) MR2049 "That's Why I'm Blue" only

Regal-Zonophone (UK) T5724

Zonophone (UK) 5724

VICTOR 22488

    Own, vocal, guitar; Acc. unknown, violin; unknown, clarinet; unknown, cornet; unknown, piano; unknown, tuba; unknown, traps;

    New York City   February 21, 1929

    48385-1   Any Old Time

VICTOR 22488

    Own, vocal, guitar; Acc. Billy Burkes, guitar

    Atlanta, Georgia   November 26, 1929

    56607-1   Anniversary Blue Yodel (Blue Yodel No. 7)

Bluebird B-5664 "Any Old Time" only

Montgomery Ward M-4210 "Anniversary Blue Yodel (Blue Yodel No. 7)" only

Montgomery Ward M-4730 "Any Old Time" only

Zonophone (Australia) EE221 "Any Old Time" only

Regal-Zonophone (UK) T5780

Zonophone (UK) 5780

VICTOR 22523

    Own, vocal, guitar;
    New York City   February 23, 1929
    49991-2   High Powered Mama

VICTOR 22523

    Own, vocal, guitar;
    Hollywood, California   July 12, 1930
    54864-1   In The Jail-House Now – No. 2

Montgomery Ward M-4315
Victor (Reissue) 20-6092 "In The Jail-House Now – No. 2" only
Regal-Zonophone (Australia) T5808
Regal-Zonophone (Ireland) IZ334
Zonophone (UK) 5808

VICTOR 22554

    Own, vocal, yodel, guitar;
    Hollywood, California   July 1, 1930
    54852-2   Pistol Packin' Papa

VICTOR 22554

    Acc. Lani McIntire, guitar;
    Hollywood, California   July 5, 1930
    54855-1   Those Gambler's Blues

Montgomery Ward M-4211 "Those Gambler's Blues" only
Montgomery Ward M-4316, M-4730 "Pistol Packin' Papa" only
Regal-Zonophone / Zonophone (Australia) EE232
Regal-Zonophone (UK) MR911 "Those Gambler's Blues" only
Regal-Zonophone (UK) T6011 "Pistol Packin' Papa" only
Zonophone (UK) 6011 "Pistol Packin' Papa" only

VICTOR 23503

    Acc. Bob Sawyer's Jazz Band; unknown, cornet; unknown, clarinet; Bob Sawyer, piano; unknown, banjo; unknown, tuba;

    Hollywood, California   July 10, 1930

    54861-3   Jimmie's Mean Mama Blues

VICTOR 23503

    Own, guitar; Acc. Bob Sawyer's Jazz Band; unknown, cornet; unknown, clarinet; Bob Sawyer, piano; unknown, banjo; unknown, tuba;

    Hollywood, California   July 11, 1930

    54863-1   Blue Yodel No. 8 (Mule Skinner Blues)

Bluebird B-6275 "Jimmie's Mean Mama Blues" only

Montgomery Ward M-4723

Montgomery Ward M-8235 "Blue Yodel No. 8 (Mule Skinner Blues)" only

Victor (Reissue) 20-6205 "Blue Yodel No. 8 (Mule Skinner Blues)" only

Regal-Zonophone (Australia) G23115

HMV (Australia) EA1541

Regal-Zonophone / Zonophone (UK) T5859 / 5859

VICTOR 23518

    Acc. Billy Burkes, guitar

    Atlanta, Georgia   November 25, 1929

    56595-4   Nobody Knows But Me

VICTOR 23518

    Own, vocal, guitar, effects

    Hollywood, California   July 11, 1930

    54862-3   The Mystery Of Number Five

Bluebird B-5739 "The Mystery Of Number Five" only

Montgomery Ward M-4223 "The Mystery Of Number Five" only

Regal-Zonophone (Australia) G23198

HMV (Australia) EA 1401

Regal-Zonophone (Ireland) IZ401 "The Mystery Of Number Five" only

Regal-Zonophone (UK) MR 1599 "The Mystery Of Number Five" only

VICTOR 23535

    Acc. Billy Burkes, guitar

    Atlanta, Georgia   November 25, 1929

    56594-3   Mississippi River Blues

VICTOR 23535

    Own, vocal, yodel, guitar; Acc. Charles Kama, steel guitar

    San Antonio, Texas   January 31, 1931

    67133-3   T.B. Blues

Bluebird B-5393 "Mississippi River Blues" only

Bluebird B-6275 "T.B. Blues" only

Montgomery Ward M-4067, M-4729 "T.B. Blues" only

Montgomery Ward M-4722 "Mississippi River Blues" only

Regal-Zonophone (Australia) G23199

HMV (Australia) EA 1402

Regal-Zonophone (Ireland) IZ 616 "T.B. Blues" only

Regal-Zonophone (UK) MR 911, MR 2374 "T.B. Blues" only

Regal-Zonophone (UK) T5983 "Mississippi River Blues" only

Zonophone (UK) 5983 "Mississippi River Blues" only

VICTOR 23549

    Acc. Bob Sawyer's Jazz Band; unknown, cornet; unknown, clarinet; Bob Sawyer, piano; unknown, banjo; unknown, tuba;

    Hollywood, California   June 30, 1930

    54849-2   My Blue Eyed Jane

VICTOR 23549

    Acc. Charles Kama, steel guitar; M.T. Salazar, guitar; Mike Cordova, string bass;

    San Antonio, Texas   January 31, 1931

    67135-1   Jimmie The Kid (Parts Of The Life Of Rodgers)

Bluebird B-5393 "My Blue Eyed Jane" only

Montgomery Ward M-4222 "My Blue Eyed Jane" only

Montgomery Ward M-4731 "Jimmie The Kid (Parts Of The Life Of Rodgers)" only

Regal-Zonophone (Australia) G23196

HMV (Australia) EA 1339 "My Blue Eyed Jane" only

Regal-Zonophone (UK) T6022, MR3208 "Jimmie The Kid (Parts Of The Life Of Rodgers)" only

Zonophone (UK)6022 "Jimmie The Kid (Parts Of The Life Of Rodgers)" only

VICTOR 23564

    Own, vocal; Acc. Lani McIntire's Hawaiian's; Sam Koki, steel guitar; Lani McIntire, guitar; unknown, ukulele; unknown, string bass;

    Hollywood, California   July 7, 1930

    54856-2   I'm Lonesome Too

VICTOR 23564

    Acc. Shelly Lee Alley, fiddle; Alvin Alley, fiddle; Charles Kama, steel guitar; M.T. Salazar, guitar; Mike Cordova, string bass;

    San Antonio, Texas   January 31, 1931

    67134-2   Travellin' Blues

Bluebird B-5739 "I'm Lonesome Too" only

Montgomery Ward M-4220 "I'm Lonesome Too" only

Montgomery Ward M-4729 "Travellin' Blues" only

Regal-Zonophone (Australia) G23112 "Travellin' Blues" only

Regal-Zonophone (Australia) G23189 "I'm Lonesome Too" only

HMV (Australia) EA1253 "I'm Lonesome Too" only

HMV (Australia) EA 1514 "Travellin' Blues" only

Regal-Zonophone (Ireland) IZ401 "I'm Lonesome Too" only

Regal-Zonophone (UK) MR1599 "I'm Lonesome Too" only

VICTOR 23574

    Acc. Lani McIntire's Hawaiian's; Sam Koki, steel guitar; Lani McIntire, guitar; unknown, ukulele; unknown, string bass;

    Hollywood, California   June 30, 1930

    54851-3   Moonlight And Skies

VICTOR 23574 (as by "Jimmie Rodgers (Assisted By The Carter Family)")

    Own, vocal, yodel, speaking; Sara Carter, vocal, speaking, guitar; A.P. Carter, vocal, speaking; Maybelle Carter, vocal, speaking, mandolin, guitar;

    Louisville, Kentucky   June 12, 1931

    69427-4   Jimmie Rodgers Visits The Carter Family

Bluebird B-5000 "Moonlight And Skies" only

Electradisk 1830, 1958 "Moonlight And Skies" only

Montgomery Ward M-4216 "Moonlight And Skies" only

Montgomery Ward M-4720

Regal-Zonophone / Zonophone (Australia) EE369

Columbia (Ireland) IFB341 "Moonlight And Skies" only

Regal-Zonophone (Ireland) IZ469 "Moonlight And Skies" only

Regal-Zonophone (UK) MR2200 "Moonlight And Skies" only

Regal-Zonophone (UK) ME34, MR3164 "Jimmie Rodgers Visits The Carter Family" only

VICTOR 23580

    Acc. Louis Armstrong, trumpet; Lillian Hardin Armstrong, piano;

    Hollywood, California   July 16, 1930

    54867-2   Blue Yodel No. 9

VICTOR 23580

    Own, ukulele; Acc. Cliff Carlisle, steel guitar; Wilbur Ball, guitar;

    Louisville, Kentucky   June 15, 1931

    69443-3   Looking For A New Mama

Bluebird B-5037 "Looking For A New Mama" only

Electradisk 1966 "Looking For A New Mama" only

Montgomery Ward M-4203 "Looking For A New Mama" only

Montgomery Ward M-4209. M-4724 "Blue Yodel No. 9" only

Sunrise S-3131 "Looking For A New Mama" only

Regal-Zonophone / Zonophone (Australia) EE300

Regal-Zonophone (UK) ME15, MR3002 "Looking For A New Mama" only

Regal-Zonophone (UK) MR3208 "Blue Yodel No. 9" only

VICTOR 23609

    Own, vocal, yodel;   Acc. Lani McIntire's Hawaiian's; Sam Koki, steel guitar; Lani McIntire, guitar; unknown, ukulele; unknown, string bass;

    Hollywood, California   June 30, 1930

    54850-3   Why Should I Be Lonely

VICTOR 23609

    Acc. Ruth Ann Moore, piano;

    Louisville, Kentucky   June 16, 1931

    69448-1   What's It?

Bluebird B-5082 "Why Should I Be Lonely" only

Bluebird B-5084 "What's It?" only

Montgomery Ward M-4204 "Why Should I Be Lonely" only

Montgomery Ward M-4208 "What's It?" only

Sunrise S-3169 "Why Should I Be Lonely" only

Sunrise S-3171 "What's It?" only

Regal-Zonophone / Zonophone (Australia) EE305

Regal-Zonophone (Ireland) IZ336 "Why Should I Be Lonely" only

Regal-Zonophone (UK) T6102 "Why Should I Be Lonely" only

Zonophone (UK) 6102 "Why Should I Be Lonely" only

❖   Zonophone (UK) 6102 as by "Jimmy Rodgers"

VICTOR 23621

    Own, vocal, yodel, guitar;

    Louisville, Kentucky   July 11, 1931

    69424-3   Let Me Be Your Side Track

VICTOR 23621

    Own, vocal, yodel, guitar;

    Camden, New Jersey   November 11, 1931

    69032-3   Rodgers' Puzzle Record

❖   *69302-3 was a combination of tracks "Train Whistle Blues", "Blue Yodel" and "Everybody Does It In Hawaii" which were remastered and pressed onto side two of VICTOR 23621 and titled "Rodgers' Puzzle Record"*

Montgomery Ward M-4209 "Let Me Be Your Side Track" only

Sunrise S-3171 "Let Me Be Your Side Track" only

Regal-Zonophone (Australia) G23204 "Rodgers' Puzzle Record" only

Regal-Zonophone / Zonophone (Australia) EE363 "Let Me Be Your Side Track" only

HMV (Australia) EA1489 "Rodgers' Puzzle Record" only

Regal-Zonophone (UK) T6056

Zonophone (UK) 6056

❖ Zonophone 6056 as by "Jimmy Rodgers"

VICTOR 23636

Own, vocal, yodel; Acc. Cliff Carlisle, steel guitar; Wilbur Ball, guitar;

Louisville, Kentucky　　　　　　　　　　June 13, 1931

69432-2　　　　　　　　　　When The Cactus Is In Bloom

VICTOR 23636

Acc. Ruth Ann Moore, piano;

Louisville, Kentucky　　　　　　　　　　June 15, 1931

69439-2　　　　　　　　　　Gambling Polka Dot Blues

Bluebird B-5163 "When The Cactus Is In Bloom" only

Electradisk 2060 "When The Cactus Is In Bloom" only

Montgomery Ward M-4216 "When The Cactus Is In Bloom" only

Sunrise S-3244 "When The Cactus Is In Bloom" only

Regal-Zonophone / Zonophone (Australia) EE345

Regal-Zonophone (UK) MR2795 "When The Cactus Is In Bloom" only

❖ Regal-Zonophone (UK) MR2795 titled as *"Round Up Time Out West (When The Cactus Is In Bloom"*

❖ Some issues of Regal-Zonophone / Zonophone (Australia) possibly titled as *"Round Up Time Out West (When The Cactus Is In Bloom"*

VICTOR 23651

Own, vocal, yodel; Acc. Lani McIntire's Hawaiian's; Sam Koki, steel guitar; Lani McIntire, guitar; unknown, ukulele; unknown, string bass;

Hollywood, California   July 9, 1930

54860-3   For The Sake Of Days Gone By

VICTOR 23651

Own, vocal, yodel; Acc. Dick Bunyard, steel guitar; Red Young, mandolin; Bill Boyd, guitar' Fred Koone, string bass;

Dallas, Texas   February 2, 1932

70645-2   Roll Along Kentucky Moon

Bluebird B-5082 "Roll Along Kentucky Moon" only

Bluebird B-5784 "For The Sake Of Days Gone By" only

Montgomery Ward M-4219 "Roll Along Kentucky Moon" only

Montgomery Ward M-4221 "For The Sake Of Days Gone By" only

Sunrise S-3169 "Roll Along Kentucky Moon" only

Regal-Zonophone (Australia) G23188 "Roll Along Kentucky Moon" only

Regal-Zonophone / Zonophone (Australia) EE363 "For The Sake Of Days Gone By" only

HMV (Australia) EA1228 "Roll Along Kentucky Moon" only

Regal-Zonophone (Ireland) IZ1004 "Roll Along Kentucky Moon" only

Regal-Zonophone (UK) MR3122 "Roll Along Kentucky Moon" only

Victor (Japan) A1430

VICTOR 23669

Own, guitar; Acc. Billy Burkes, steel guitar; Weldon Burkes, guitar; Fred Koone, string bass;

Dallas, Texas   February 4, 1932

70647-3   My Time Ain't Long

VICTOR 23669

Own, guitar, vocal effects; Acc. Billy Burkes, guitar; Weldon Burkes, guitar; Fred Koone, string bass; Charlie Burkes, ukulele;

Dallas, Texas   February 4, 1932

70648-2   Ninety Nine Years Blues

Bluebird B-5083 "My Time Ain't Long" only

Electradisk 2009 "My Time Ain't Long" only

Montgomery Ward M-4215 "Ninety Nine Years Blues" only

Sunrise S-3170 "My Time Ain't Long" only

Regal-Zonophone (Australia) / (UK) T6159

Zonophone (Australia) / (UK) 6159

VICTOR 23681

    Own, vocal, guitar;

    Atlanta, Georgia   November 26, 1929

    56608-1   She Was Happy Till She Met You

VICTOR 23681

    Own, guitar; Acc. Joe Kaipo, steel guitar;

    Dallas, Texas   August 12, 1929

    55345-4   Home Call

Bluebird B-5057 "She Was Happy Till She Met You" only

Electradisk 1983 "She Was Happy Till She Met You" only

Montgomery Ward M-4207, M-4324 "She Was Happy Till She Met You" only

Sunrise S-3142 "She Was Happy Till She Met You" only

Regal-Zonophone / Zonophone (Australia) EE352

Regal-Zonophone (Ireland) IZ388

Regal-Zonophone (UK) MR 1355

❖ It is unclear whether or not "Home Call" 55345-4 is on the reverse of any the "Regal-Zonophone" copies – it is known that "Take 2" and "Take 3" were unissued as 78 RPM records and can be found in the "Unissued" section of this book.

VICTOR 23696

    Own, guitar; Acc. Billy Burkes, steel guitar; Weldon Burkes, guitar; Fred Koone, string bass;

    Dallas, Texas   February 4, 1932

    45091-5   Mississippi Moon

VICTOR 23696

Own, guitar;

Dallas, Texas　　　　　　　　　　　　　　　February 6, 1932

70650-1　Blue Yodel No. 10 (Ground Hog Rootin' In My Back Yard)

Bluebird B-5136 "Mississippi Moon" only

Electradisk 2042 "Mississippi Moon" only

Montgomery Ward M-4208, M-4725 "Blue Yodel No. 10 (Ground Hog Rootin' In My Back Yard)" only

Montgomery Ward M-4220 "Mississippi Moon" only

Sunrise S-3217 "Mississippi Moon" only

Regal-Zonophone (Australia) G23189 "Mississippi Moon" only

HMV (Australia) EA1253 "Mississippi Moon" only

Regal-Zonophone (Ireland) IZ410 "Mississippi Moon" only

Regal-Zonophone (UK) MR1853 "Mississippi Moon" only

Regal-Zonophone (UK) MR3257 "Blue Yodel No. 10 (Ground Hog Rootin' In My Back Yard)" only

Victor (Japan) A1401, JA708

VICTOR 23711

Acc. Dick Bunyard, steel guitar; Red Young, mandolin; Bill Boyd, guitar; Fred Koone, string bass;

Dallas, Texas　　　　　　　　　　　　　　　February 3, 1932

70646-1　　　　　　　　　　　　　　　Hobo's Meditation

VICTOR 23711

Own, guitar; Acc. Fred Koone, guitar;

Dallas, Texas　　　　　　　　　　　　　　　February 5, 1932

70649-1　　　　　　　　　　　Down The Old Road To Home

Bluebird B-5081 "Down The Old Road To Home" only

Montgomery Ward M-4202 "Down The Old Road To Home" only

Montgomery Ward M-4205 "Hobo's Meditation" only

Regal-Zonophone (Australia) G23192

HMV (Australia) EA1374

Regal-Zonophone (Ireland) IZ404 "Down The Old Road To Home" only

Regal-Zonophone (Ireland) IZ1065 "Hobo's Meditation" only

Regal_Zonophone (UK) MR1725 "Down The Old Road To Home" only

Regal-Zonophone (UK) MR3313 "Hobo's Meditation" only

VICTOR 23721
    Acc. Clayton McMichen, fiddle; Oddie McWinders, banjo; Hoyt "Slim" Bryant, guitar;

    Camden, New Jersey   August 11, 1932

    58961-2A   Mother, Queen Of My Heart

VICTOR 23721
    Acc. Clayton McMichen, fiddle; Oddie McWinders, banjo; Hoyt "Slim" Bryant, guitar;

    Camden, New Jersey   August 11, 1932

    58963-1A   Rock All Our Babies To Sleep

Bluebird B-5000 "Rock All Our Babies To Sleep" only

Bluebird B-5080 "Mother, Queen Of My Heart" only

Electradisk 1830 "Rock All Our Babies To Sleep" only

Electradisk 2008 "Mother, Queen Of My Heart" only

Montgomery Ward M-4201 "Rock All Our Babies To Sleep" only

Montgomery Ward M-4206 "Mother, Queen Of My Heart" only

Sunrise S-3104 "Rock All Our Babies To Sleep" only

Sunrise S-3167 "Mother, Queen Of My Heart" only

Victor (Reissue) 20-6205 "Mother, Queen Of My Heart" only

Regal-Zonophone (Australia) G23195 "Mother, Queen Of My Heart" only

Regal-Zonophone (Australia) G23200 "Rock All Our Babies To Sleep" only

HMV (Australia) EA1390 "Mother, Queen Of My Heart" only

HMV (Australia) EA1403 "Rock All Our Babies To Sleep" only

Columbia (Ireland) IFB341 "Rock All Our Babies To Sleep" only

Regal-Zonophone (Ireland) IZ469 "Rock All Our Babies To Sleep" only

Regal-Zonophone (UK) MR1310 "Mother, Queen Of My Heart" only

Regal-Zonophone (UK) MR2200 "Rock All Our Babies To Sleep" only

VICTOR 23736

Acc. unknown, fiddle; unknown, fiddle; unknown, clarinet; unknown, piano; Hoyt "Slim" Bryant, guitar;

New York City   August 29, 1932

73324-1   In The Hills Of Tennessee

73326-1   Miss The Mississippi And You

Bluebird B-5081 Miss The Mississippi And You

Bluebird B-5784 "In The Hills Of Tennessee" only

Montgomery Ward M-4200 "In The Hills Of Tennessee" only

Montgomery Ward M-4206 Miss The Mississippi And You

Sunrise S-3168 Miss The Mississippi And You

Regal-Zonophone (Australia) G23201

HMV (Australia) EA1404

Regal-Zonophone (UK) MR2700 "In The Hills Of Tennessee" only

Regal-Zonophone (UK) MR3257 "Miss The Mississippi And You" only

VICTOR 23751

Acc. Clayton McMichen, fiddle; Oddie McWinders, banjo; Hoyt "Slim" Bryant, guitar;

Camden, New Jersey   August 11, 1932

58964-1   Whippin' That Old T.B.

VICTOR 23751

Own, guitar; Acc. Clayton McMichen, fiddle; Hoyt "Slim" Bryant, guitar;

Camden, New Jersey   August 15, 1932

58968-2A   No Hard Times

Bluebird B-5076 "Whippin' That Old T.B." only

Electradisk 1999 "Whippin' That Old T.B." only

Montgomery Ward M-4204 "Whippin' That Old T.B." only

Montgomery Ward M-4205 "No Hard Times" only

Sunrise S-3157 "Whippin' That Old T.B." only

Regal-Zonophone (Australia) G23117 "No Hard Times" only

Regal-Zonophone (Australia) G23195 "Whippin' That Old T.B." only

HMV (Australia) EA1390 "Whippin' That Old T.B." only

HMV (Australia) EA1534 "No Hard Times" only

Regal-Zonophone (UK) MR1310 "Whippin' That Old T.B." only

VICTOR 23766

    Own, guitar; Acc. Oddie McWinders, banjo;

    Camden, New Jersey   August 15, 1932

    58969-1A   Long Tall Mamma Blues

VICTOR 23766

    Acc. Clayton McMichen, fiddle; Oddie McWinders, banjo; Hoyt "Slim" Bryant, guitar;

    Camden, New Jersey   August 16, 1932

    58971-3   Gambling Barroom Blues

Bluebird B-5037 "Gambling Barroom Blues" only

Electradisk 1966 "Gambling Barroom Blues" only

Montgomery Ward M-4202 "Long Tall Mamma Blues" only

Montgomery Ward M-4203 "Gambling Barroom Blues" only

Sunrise S-3131 "Gambling Barroom Blues" only

Regal-Zonophone (Australia) G23112 "Gambling Barroom Blues" only

HMV (Australia) EA1514 "Gambling Barroom Blues" only

Regal-Zonophone (UK) ME15, MR3002 "Gambling Barroom Blues" only

VICTOR 23781

    Acc. Clayton McMichen, fiddle; Oddie McWinders, banjo; Hoyt "Slim" Bryant, guitar;

    Camden, New Jersey   August 15, 1932

    58970-2A   Peach Pickin' Time Down In Georgia

VICTOR 23781

    Acc. unknown, fiddle; unknown, fiddle; unknown, clarinet; unknown, piano; Hoyt "Slim" Bryant, guitar;

    New York City   August 29, 1932

    73325-1   Prairie Lullaby

Bluebird B-5076 "Prairie Lullaby" only

Bluebird B-5080 "Peach Pickin' Time Down In Georgia" only

Electradisk 1999 "Prairie Lullaby" only

Electradisk 2008 "Peach Pickin' Time Down In Georgia" only

Montgomery Ward M-4200 "Peach Pickin' Time Down In Georgia" only

Montgomery Ward M-4201 "Prairie Lullaby" only

Sunrise S-3157 "Prairie Lullaby" only

Sunrise S-3167 "Peach Pickin' Time Down In Georgia" only

Victor (Reissue) 20-6092 "Peach Pickin' Time Down In Georgia" only

Regal-Zonophone (Australia) G23200 "Peach Pickin' Time Down In Georgia" only

Regal-Zonophone (Australia) G23203 "Prairie Lullaby" only

HMV (Australia) EA1403 "Peach Pickin' Time Down In Georgia" only

HMV (Australia) EA1405 "Prairie Lullaby" only

Regal-Zonophone (Ireland) IZ388 "Peach Pickin' Time Down In Georgia" only

Regal-Zonophone (Ireland) IZ404 "Prairie Lullaby" only

Regal-Zonophone (UK) MR1335

Regal-Zonophone (UK) MR1725 "Prairie Lullaby" only

VICTOR 23796

Own, vocal, guitar; Billy Burkes, guitar

Atlanta, Georgia   November 27, 1929

56617-1   Blue Yodel Number Eleven

VICTOR 23796

Acc. Hoyt "Slim" Bryant, guitar; unknown, fiddle; unknown, fiddle; unknown, clarinet; unknown, piano;

New York City   August 29, 1932

73327-1   Sweet Mama Hurry Home Or I'll Be Gone

Montgomery Ward M-4726

Regal-Zonophone (Australia) G23202 "Sweet Mama Hurry Home Or I'll Be Gone" only

HMV (Australia) EA 1406 "Sweet Mama Hurry Home Or I'll Be Gone" only

VICTOR 23811

    Own, guitar;

    Dallas, Texas   October 22, 1929

    56450-1   The Land Of My Boyhood Dreams

VICTOR 23811

    Own, guitar;

    Louisville, Kentucky   June 16, 1931

    69458-1   Southern Cannon-Ball

Bluebird B-5337 "The Land Of My Boyhood Dreams" only

Montgomery Ward M- 4450 "The Land Of My Boyhood Dreams" only

Montgomery Ward M-4728

Regal-Zonophone (Australia) G23111 "Southern Cannon-Ball" only

Regal-Zonophone (Australia) G23190 "The Land Of My Boyhood Dreams"

HMV (Australia) EA 1303 "The Land Of My Boyhood Dreams" only

HMV (Australia) EA 1503 "Southern Cannon-Ball" only

VICTOR 23816

    Own, guitar;

    New York City   May 20, 1933

    76192-1   Old Pal Of My Heart

VICTOR 23816

    Acc. John Cali, banjo; Tony Colicchio, guitar;

    New York City   May 24, 1933

    76328-1   Mississippi Delta Blues

Bluebird B-5136 "Old Pal Of My Heart" only

Electradisk 2042 "Old Pal Of My Heart" only

Sunrise S-3217 "Old Pal Of My Heart" only

Regal-Zonophone (Australia) G23191 "Old Pal Of My Heart" only

Regal-Zonophone (Australia) G23194 "Mississippi Delta Blues" only

HMV (Australia) EA1362 "Old Pal Of My Heart" only

HMV (Australia) EA1385 "Mississippi Delta Blues" only

Regal-Zonophone (Ireland) IZ496 "Old Pal Of My Heart" only

Regal-Zonophone (UK) MR2242 "Old Pal Of My Heart" only

VICTOR 23830

    Own, guitar;

    New York City   May 17, 1933

    76141-1   I'm Free (From The Chain Gang Now)

VICTOR 23830

    Own, guitar;

    New York City   May 20, 1933

    76191-1   The Yodeling Ranger

Bluebird B-5556 "The Yodeling Ranger" only

Montgomery Ward M-4453

Regal-Zonophone (Australia) G23203 "The Yodeling Ranger" only

Regal-Zonophone (Australia) G23204 "I'm Free (From The Chain Gang Now)" only

HMV (Australia) EA1405 "The Yodeling Ranger" only

HMV (Australia) EA 1489 "I'm Free (From The Chain Gang Now)" only

Regal-Zonophone (Ireland) IZ410 "The Yodeling Ranger" only

Regal-Zonophone (UK) MR1853 "The Yodeling Ranger" only

VICTOR 23840

    Acc. John Cali, steel guitar; Tony Colicchio, guitar;

    New York City   May 24, 1933

    76327-1   Old Love Letters (Bring Memories Of You)

VICTOR 23840

    Acc. John Cali, guitar; Tony Colicchio, guitar;

    New York City   May 24, 1933

    76331-1   Somewhere Down Below The Dixon Line

Bluebird B-6198 "Old Love Letters (Bring Memories Of You)" only

Montgomery Ward M-4454

Regal-Zonophone (Australia) G23111 "Somewhere Down Below The Dixon Line" only

Regal-Zonophone (Australia) G23190 "Old Love Letters (Bring Memories Of You)" only

HMV (Australia) EA1053 "Somewhere Down Below The Dixon Line" only

HMV (Australia) EA1303 "Old Love Letters (Bring Memories Of You)" only

Regal-Zonophone (Ireland) IZ422 "Old Love Letters (Bring Memories Of You)" only

Regal-Zonophone (UK) MR2049 "Old Love Letters (Bring Memories Of You)" only

VICTOR 24456

    Own, guitar;

    New York City   May 17, 1933

    76138-1   Blue Yodel No. 12

    76140-1   The Cow Hand's Last Ride

Montgomery Ward M-4727

Victor 18-6000 (Picture Disc) – *See listing at end of this section*

Regal-Zonophone (Australia) G23191 "The Cow Hand's Last Ride" only

HMV (Australia) EA1362 "The Cow Hand's Last Ride" only

VICTOR V-40014

    Own, vocal; Acc. C.L. Hutchison, cornet; James Rikard, clarinet; John Westbrook, steel guitar; Dean Bryan, guitar; George MacMillan, string bass

    Atlanta, Georgia   October 20, 1928

    47216-4   Blue Yodel No. 4 (California Blues)

VICTOR V-40014

    Own, vocal, vocal effects; Acc. C.L. Hutchison, cornet; James Rikard, clarinet; John Westbrook, steel guitar; Dean Bryan, guitar; George MacMillan, string bass

    Atlanta, Georgia   October 22, 1928

    47223-4   Waiting For A Train

Bluebird B-5163 "Waiting For A Train" only

Electradisk 2060 "Waiting For A Train" only

Montgomery Ward M-4722, M-8124 "Blue Yodel No. 4 (California Blues)" only

Montgomery Ward M-8109 "Waiting For A Train" only

Sunrise S-3244 "Waiting For A Train" only

Victor (Reissue) 21-0175

Regal-Zonophone (Australia) T5380

Zonophone (Australia) 5380

Regal-Zonophone (Ireland) IZ320

Regal-Zonophone (UK) T5380

Zonophone (UK) 5380

VICTOR V-40054

Own, vocal, yodel, guitar; Acc. The Three Southerners; Ellsworth T. Cozzens, steel guitar; Julian R. Ninde, guitar

Camden, New Jersey   February 14, 1928

41739-1   The Sailor's Plea

VICTOR V-40054

Own, vocal; Acc. C.L. Hutchison, cornet; John Westbrook, steel guitar; Dean Bryan, guitar; George MacMillan, string bass

Atlanta, Georgia   October 22, 1928

47224-3   I'm Lonely And Blue

47224-5   I'm Lonely And Blue

Matrix 47224-3 is on earlier issues of Victor V-40054 only

Bluebird B-6246, 33-0513 "The Sailor's Plea" only

Montgomery Ward M-4047, M-4217 " I'm Lonely And Blue" only

Montgomery Ward M-5036 "The Sailor's Plea" only

Regal-Zonophone (Australia) T5401

Zonophone (Australia)

Regal Zonophone (Ireland) IZ321 "

Regal-Zonophone (UK) T5401

Zonophone (UK) 5401

VICTOR V-40072

Own, vocal, guitar;

Camden, New Jersey   June 12, 1928

45094-1   You And My Old Guitar

45096-1   My Little Lady

Bluebird B-5083" You And My Old Guitar" only

Bluebird B-5838 "My Little Lady" only

Electradisk 2009 " You And My Old Guitar" only

Montgomery Ward M-4224 " You And My Old Guitar" only

Montgomery Ward M-4731 "My Little Lady" only

Sunrise S-3170 " You And My Old Guitar" only

Regal-Zonophone (Australia) T5423

Zonophone (Australia) 5423

Regal-Zonophone (Ireland) IZ323

Regal-Zonophone (UK) T5423

Zonophone (UK) 5423

VICTOR V-40096

Own, vocal; Acc. C.L. Hutchison, cornet; James Rikard, clarinet; John Westbrook, steel guitar; Dean Bryan, guitar; George MacMillan, string bass

Atlanta, Georgia   October 20, 1928

47215-3   My Carolina Sunshine Girl

VICTOR V-40096

Own, vocal; Acc. unknown, violin; unknown, clarinet; unknown, cornet; unknown, piano; unknown, tuba; unknown, traps;

New York City   February 21, 1929

48384-3   Desert Blues

Bluebird B-5556 "My Carolina Sunshine Girl" only

Montgomery Ward M-4451

Victor (Reissue) 21-0176 "Desert Blues" only

Victor (Reissue) 21-0180 "My Carolina Sunshine Girl" only

Regal-Zonophone (Australia) T5495

Zonophone (Australia) 5495

Regal-Zonophone (UK) T5495

Zonophone (UK) 5495

VICTOR 18-6000 (Picture Disc)
    Own, guitar;
    New York City   May 17, 1933
    76138-1   Blue Yodel No. 12
    76140-1   The Cow Hand's Last Ride

❖ 18-6000 is a picture disc that was released in June of 1933 about one month after the untimely death of Jimmie Rodgers. The tracks are taken from the original issued record 24456.

BLUEBIRD 78 RPM - Label Releases

Bluebird was a subsequent label that released Jimmie Rodgers' original Victor record label recordings in the 1930's. You will find in this section each record's information and which original VICTOR record it was originally issued.

Bluebird also released some Jimmie Rodger's tracks that were not released on the Victor label – if there is not a Victor listing below the record information then it was not released on the Victor label first but on the Bluebird label. (Some tracks were reissued on to the Victor label at a later date).

Also listed below the record information are the foreign listings - however they are only listed for the Bluebird first releases, all other foreign listings can be found in the VICTOR Label Listings section of this book.

BLUEBIRD B-5000
    Acc. Lani McIntire's Hawaiian's; Sam Koki, steel guitar; Lani McIntire, guitar; unknown, ukulele; unknown, string bass;
    Hollywood, California   June 30, 1930
    54851-3   Moonlight And Skies

BLUEBIRD B-5000
    Acc. Clayton McMichen, fiddle; Oddie McWinders, banjo; Hoyt "Slim" Bryant, guitar;
    Camden, New Jersey   August 11, 1932
    58963-1A   Rock All Our Babies To Sleep

Victor 23574 "Moonlight And Skies" only
Victor 23721 "Rock All Our Babies To Sleep" only

BLUEBIRD B-5037

    Own, ukulele; Acc. Cliff Carlisle, steel guitar; Wilbur Ball, guitar;

    Louisville, Kentucky   June 15, 1931

    69443-3   Looking For A New Mama

BLUEBIRD B-5037

    Acc. Clayton McMichen, fiddle; Oddie McWinders, banjo; Hoyt "Slim" Bryant, guitar;

    Camden, New Jersey   August 16, 1932

    58971-3   Gambling Barroom Blues

Victor 23580 "Looking For A New Mama" only

Victor 23766 "Gambling Barroom Blues" only

BLUEBIRD B-5057

    Acc. Joe Kaipo, steel guitar; Billy Burkes, guitar; Weldon Burkes, ukulele

    Dallas, Texas   October 22, 1929

    56449-3   Whisper Your Mother's Name

BLUEBIRD B-5057

    Own, vocal, guitar;

    Atlanta, Georgia   November 26, 1929

    56608-1   She Was Happy Till She Met You

Victor 22319 "Whisper Your Mother's Name" only

Victor 23681 "She Was Happy Till She Met You" only

BLUEBIRD B-5076

    Acc. Clayton McMichen, fiddle; Oddie McWinders, banjo; Hoyt "Slim" Bryant, guitar;

    Camden, New Jersey   August 11, 1932

    58964-1   Whippin' That Old T.B.

BLUEBIRD B-5076

    Acc. unknown, fiddle; unknown, fiddle; unknown, clarinet; unknown, piano; Hoyt "Slim" Bryant, guitar;

    New York City   August 29, 1932

    73325-1   Prairie Lullaby

Victor 23751 "Whippin' That Old T.B." only

Victor 23781 "Prairie Lullaby" only

BLUEBIRD B-5080
    Acc. Clayton McMichen, fiddle; Oddie McWinders, banjo; Hoyt "Slim" Bryant, guitar;

    Camden, New Jersey   August 11, 1932

    58961-2A   Mother, Queen Of My Heart

BLUEBIRD B-5080
    Acc. Clayton McMichen, fiddle; Oddie McWinders, banjo; Hoyt "Slim" Bryant, guitar;

    Camden, New Jersey   August 15, 1932

    58970-2A   Peach Pickin' Time Down In Georgia

Victor 23721 "Mother, Queen Of My Heart" only

Victor 23781 "Peach Pickin' Time Down In Georgia" only

BLUEBIRD B-5081
    Own, guitar; Acc. Fred Koone, guitar;

    Dallas, Texas   February 5, 1932

    70649-1   Down The Old Road To Home

BLUEBIRD B-5081
    Acc. unknown, fiddle; unknown, fiddle; unknown, clarinet; unknown, piano; Hoyt "Slim" Bryant, guitar;

    New York City   August 29, 1932

    73326-1   Miss The Mississippi And You

Victor 23711 "Down The Road To Home" only

Victor 23736 "Miss The Mississippi And You" only

BLUEBIRD B-5082
    Own, vocal, yodel; Acc. Lani McIntire's Hawaiian's; Sam Koki, steel guitar; Lani McIntire, guitar; unknown, ukulele; unknown, string bass;

    Hollywood, California   June 30, 1930

    54850-3   Why Should I Be Lonely

BLUEBIRD B-5082

    Own, vocal, yodel; Acc. Dick Bunyard, steel guitar; Red Young, mandolin; Bill Boyd, guitar' Fred Koone, string bass;

    Dallas, Texas   February 2, 1932

    70645-2   Roll Along Kentucky Moon

Victor 23609 "Why Should I Be Lonely" only

Victor 23651 "Roll Along Kentucky Moon" only

BLUEBIRD B-5083

    Own, vocal, guitar;

    Camden, New Jersey   June 12, 1928

    45094-1   You And My Old Guitar

BLUEBIRD B-5083

    Own, guitar; Acc. Billy Burkes, steel guitar; Weldon Burkes, guitar; Fred Koone, string bass;

    Dallas, Texas   February 4, 1932

    70647-3   My Time Ain't Long

Victor 23669 "My Time Ain't Long" only

Victor V-40072 "You And My Old Guitar" only

BLUEBIRD B-5084

    Acc. Ruth Ann Moore, piano;

    Louisville, Kentucky   June 16, 1931

    69448-1   What's It?

BLUEBIRD B-5084

    Own, vocal, yodel, guitar;

    Louisville, Kentucky   July 11, 1931

    69424-3   Let Me Be Your Side Track

Victor 23609 "What's It?" only

Victor 23621 "Let Me Be Your Side Track" only

BLUEBIRD B-5085

    Own, vocal, yodel; Own, guitar

    Camden, New Jersey   November 30, 1927

    40753-2   Blue Yodel

    40754-2   Away Out On The Mountain

Victor21142

BLUEBIRD B-5136

    Own, guitar; Acc. Billy Burkes, steel guitar; Weldon Burkes, guitar; Fred Koone, string bass;

    Dallas, Texas   February 4, 1932

    45091-5   Mississippi Moon

BLUEBIRD B-5136

    Own, guitar;

    New York City   May 20, 1933

    76192-1   Old Pal Of My Heart

Victor 23696 "Mississippi Moon" only

Victor 23816 "Old Pal Of My Heart" only

BLUEBIRD B-5163

    Own, vocal, vocal effects; Acc. C.L. Hutchison, cornet; James Rikard, clarinet; John Westbrook, steel guitar; Dean Bryan, guitar; George MacMillan, string bass

    Atlanta, Georgia   October 22, 1928

    47223-4   Waiting For A Train

BLUEBIRD B-5163

    Own, vocal, yodel; Acc. Cliff Carlisle, steel guitar; Wilbur Ball, guitar;

    Louisville, Kentucky   June 13, 1931

    69432-2   When The Cactus Is In Bloom

Victor 23636 "When The Cactus Is In Bloom" only

Victor V-40014 "Waiting For A Train" only

BLUEBIRD B-5223

    Own, vocal; Own, guitar; Ellsworth T. Cozzens, banjo

    Camden, New Jersey   February 15, 1928

    41740-1   In The Jailhouse Now

BLUEBIRD B-5223

    Own, vocal, guitar;

    Dallas, Texas   August 10, 1929

    55333-2   Frankie And Johnny

Victor 21245 *"In The Jailhouse Now"* only

Victor 22143 "Frankie And Johnny" only

BLUEBIRD B-5281

    Own, guitar;

    New York City   May 18, 1933

    76160-1   Jimmie Rodgers' Last Blue Yodel

BLUEBIRD B-5281

    Own, guitar;

    New York City   May 24, 1933

    76332-1   Years Ago

❖ Some issues of 76160 titled *"Jimmie Rogers' Last Ride"*

Regal-Zonophone (Australia) G23206

HMV (Australia) EA1567

Regal-Zonophone (Ireland) IZ1065 "Years Ago" only

Regal-Zonophone (UK) MR1702

Regal-Zonophone (UK) MR3313 "Years Ago" only

BLUEBIRD B-5337

    Own, vocal, guitar;

    Camden, New Jersey   June 12, 1928

    45098-2   Lullaby Yodel

BLUEBIRD B-5337

    Own, guitar;

    Dallas, Texas   October 22, 1929

    56450-1   The Land Of My Boyhood Dreams

Victor 21636 "Lullaby Yodel" only

Victor 23811 "The Land Of My Boyhood Dreams" only

BLUEBIRD B-5393

    Acc. Billy Burkes, guitar

    Atlanta, Georgia   November 25, 1929

    56594-3   Mississippi River Blues

BLUEBIRD B-5393

    Acc. Bob Sawyer's Jazz Band; unknown, cornet; unknown, clarinet; Bob Sawyer, piano; unknown, banjo; unknown, tuba;

    Hollywood, California   June 30, 1930

    54849-2   My Blue Eyed Jane

Victor 23535 "Mississippi River Blues" only

Victor 23549 "My Blue Eyed Jane" only

BLUEBIRD B-5482

    Own, vocal; Own, guitar

    Camden, New Jersey   November 30, 1927

    40751-2   Ben Dewberry's Final Run

    40752   My Mother Was A Lady

Victor 21245 "Ben Dewberry's Final Run" only

Victor 21433 "My Mother Was A Lady" only

BLUEBIRD B-5556

    Own, vocal; Acc. C.L. Hutchison, cornet; James Rikard, clarinet; John Westbrook, steel guitar; Dean Bryan, guitar; George MacMillan, string bass

    Atlanta, Georgia   October 20, 1928

    47215-3   My Carolina Sunshine Girl

BLUEBIRD B-5556

    Own, guitar;

    New York City   May 20, 1933

    76191-1   The Yodeling Ranger

Victor 23830 "The Yodeling Ranger" only

Victor V-40096 "My Carolina Sunshine Girl" only

BLUEBIRD B-5609

    Own, vocal, yodel, guitar

    Camden, New Jersey   June 12, 1928

    45093-1   My Little Old Home Town In New Orleans

BLUEBIRD B-5609

    Own, vocal, guitar;

    Camden, New Jersey   June 12, 1928

    45090-1   My Old Pal

Victor 21574 "My Little Old Home Down In New Orleans" only

Victor 21757 "My Old Pal" only

BLUEBIRD B-5664

    Own, vocal, guitar; Acc. unknown, violin; unknown, clarinet; unknown, cornet; unknown, piano; unknown, tuba; unknown, traps;

    New York City   February 21, 1929

    48385-1   Any Old Time

BLUEBIRD B-5664

    Own, vocal, guitar; Acc. Joe Kaipo, steel guitar; Billy Burkes, guitar; Weldon Burkes, Ukulele; Bob MacGimsey, whistle

    Dallas, Texas   August 8, 1929

    55308-1   Tuck Away My Lonesome Blues

Victor 22220 "Tuck Away My Lonesome Blues" only

Victor 22488 "Any Old Time" only

BLUEBIRD B-5739

Own, vocal; Acc. Lani McIntire's Hawaiian's; Sam Koki, steel guitar; Lani McIntire, guitar; unknown, ukulele; unknown, string bass;

Hollywood, California   July 7, 1930

54856-2   I'm Lonesome Too

BLUEBIRD B-5739

Own, vocal, guitar, effects

Hollywood, California   July 11, 1930

54862-3   The Mystery Of Number Five

Victor 23518 "The Mystery Of Number Five" only

Victor 23564 "I'm Lonesome Too" only

BLUEBIRD B-5784

Own, vocal, yodel; Acc. Lani McIntire's Hawaiian's; Sam Koki, steel guitar; Lani McIntire, guitar; unknown, ukulele; unknown, string bass;

Hollywood, California   July 9, 1930

54860-3   For The Sake Of Days Gone By

BLUEBIRD B-5784

Acc. unknown, fiddle; unknown, fiddle; unknown, clarinet; unknown, piano; Hoyt "Slim" Bryant, guitar;

New York City   August 29, 1932

73324-1   In The Hills Of Tennessee

Victor 23651 "For The Sake Of Days Gone By" only

Victor 23736 "In The Hills Of Tennessee" only

BLUEBIRD B-5838

Own, vocal, yodel; Acc. The Three Southerners; Ellsworth T. Cozzens, steel guitar; Julian R. Ninde, guitar

Camden, New Jersey   February 14, 1928

41737   Treasures Untold

BLUEBIRD B-5838

    Own, vocal, guitar;

    Camden, New Jersey   June 12, 1928

    45096-1   My Little Lady

Victor 21433 "Treasures Untold" only

Victor V-40072 "My Little Lady" only

BLUEBIRD B-5892

    Own, vocal, guitar;

    Dallas, Texas   October 22, 1929

    56456-3   I've Ranged, I've Roamed, I've Travelled

BLUEBIRD B-5892

    Acc. Billy Burkes, guitar;

    Atlanta, Georgia   November 28, 1929

    56620-3   Why Did You Give Me Your Love?

Regal-Zonophone (Australia) G23205

HMV (Australia) E1566

BLUEBIRD B-5942

    Acc. The Louisville Jug Band; Clifford Hayes, fiddle; George Allen, clarinet; Cal Smith, guitar; Freddie Smith, guitar; Earl McDonald, jug;

    Louisville, Kentucky   June 16, 1931

    69499-3   My Good Gal's Gone – Blues

Rev. by Jesse Rodgers

BLUEBIRD B-5991

    Own, vocal, guitar;

    Camden, New Jersey   June 12, 1928

    45095-1   Daddy And Home

BLUEBIRD B-5991
    Own, guitar;
    Dallas, Texas　　　　　　　　　　　　　　October 22, 1929
    56454-3　　　　　　　　　　　　　　　　Yodeling Cowboy
Victor 21757 "Daddy And Home" only
Victor 22271 "Yodeling Cowboy" only

BLUEBIRD B-6198
    Acc. Billy Burkes, guitar;
    Atlanta, Georgia　　　　　　　　　　　　November 28, 1929
    56619-1　　　　　　　　　　　　　　　That's Why I'm Blue

BLUEBIRD B-6198
    Acc. John Cali, steel guitar; Tony Colicchio, guitar;
    New York City　　　　　　　　　　　　　May 24, 1933
    76327-1　　　　Old Love Letters (Bring Memories Of You)
Victor 22421 "That's Why I'm Blue" only
Victor 23840 "Old Love Letters (Bring Memories Of You)" only

BLUEBIRD B-6225
    Own, vocal; Own, guitar
    Bristol, Tennessee　　　　　　　　　　　August 4, 1927
    39768-3　　　　　　　　　　　　　　　Sleep, Baby, Sleep

BLUEBIRD B-6225
    Own, vocal, yodel, guitar
    Camden, New Jersey　　　　　　　　　　June 12, 1928
    45099-1　　　　　　　　　　　　　　　Never No Mo' Blues
Victor 20864 "*Sleep, Baby, Sleep*" only
Victor 21531 "Never No Mo' Blues" only

BLUEBIRD B-6246

Own, vocal, yodel, ukulele; Acc. The Three Southerners; Ellsworth T. Cozzens, steel guitar, mandolin; Julian R. Ninde, guitar

Camden, New Jersey   February 14, 1928

41736-1   Dear Old Sunny South By The Sea

BLUEBIRD B-6246

Own, vocal, yodel, guitar; Acc. The Three Southerners; Ellsworth T. Cozzens, steel guitar; Julian R. Ninde, guitar

Camden, New Jersey   February 14, 1928

41739-1   The Sailor's Plea

Victor 21574 "Dear Old Sunny South By The Sea" only

Victor V-40054 "The Sailor's Plea" only

BLUEBIRD B-6275

Own, guitar; Acc. Bob Sawyer's Jazz Band; unknown, cornet; unknown, clarinet; Bob Sawyer, piano; unknown, banjo; unknown, tuba;

Hollywood, California   July 11, 1930

54863-1   Mule Skinner Blues

BLUEBIRD B-6275

Own, vocal, yodel, guitar; Acc. Charles Kama, steel guitar

San Antonio, Texas   January 31, 1931

67133-3   T.B. Blues

Victor 23503 "Blue Yodel No. 8 (Mule Skinner Blues)" only

Victor 23535 "T.B. Blues" only

BLUEBIRD B-6698 (As by "Jimmie Rodgers-Sara Carter")

Vocal, yodel duet; Acc. Maybelle Carter, guitar;

Louisville, Kentucky   June 10, 1931

69412-1   Why There's A Tear In My Eye

Rev. by Mrs. Jimmie Rodgers

Regal-Zonophone (Ireland) IZ616, IZ649

Regal-Zonophone (UK) ME33, MR2374, MR2429

BLUEBIRD B-6762 (as by "Jimmie Rodgers (Assisted By The Carter Family)")

    Own, vocal, yodel, speaking; Sara Carters, vocal, speaking, guitar; A.P. Carter, vocal, speaking; Maybelle Carter, vocal, speaking, mandolin, guitar;

    Louisville, Kentucky   June 11, 1931

    69428-4   The Carter Family And Jimmie Rodgers In Texas

Rev. by Monroe Brothers

Regal-Zonophone (UK) ME34, MR3164

BLUEBIRD B-6810 (As by "Jimmie Rodgers-Sara Carter")

    Vocal, yodel duet; Acc. Sara Carter, guitar; Maybelle Carter, guitar;

    Louisville, Kentucky   June 10, 1931

    69413-2   The Wonderful City

BLUEBIRD B-6810 (As by "Jimmie Rodgers")

    Acc. Clayton McMichen, fiddle; Oddie McWinders, banjo; Hoyt "Slim" Bryant, guitar;

    Camden, New Jersey   August 16, 1932

    58972-1   I've Only Loved Three Women

Regal-Zonophone (Australia) G23184

Regal-Zonophone (Ireland) IZ662

Regal-Zonophone (UK) MR2455

BLUEBIRD B-7280

    Own, vocal, yodel; Acc. Lani McIntire's Hawaiian's; Sam Koki, steel guitar; Lani McIntire, guitar; unknown, ukulele; unknown, string bass;

    Hollywood, California   July 7, 1930

    54857-1   The One Rose (That's Left In My Heart)

BLUEBIRD B-7280

    Own, guitar;

    New York City   May 18, 1933

    76151-1   Yodeling My Way Back Home

Regal-Zonophone (UK) MR2700 "Yodeling My Way Back Home" only

BLUEBIRD B-7600

    Acc. Lani McIntire's Hawaiians; Sam Koki, steel guitar; Lani McIntire, guitar; unknown, ukulele; unknown, string bass;

    Hollywood, California   July 2, 1930

    54854-3   Take Me Back Again

BLUEBIRD B-7600

    Own, guitar;

    New York City   May 17, 1933

    76139-1   Dreaming With Tears In My Eyes

BLUEBIRD 33-0513

    Own, vocal; Own, guitar

    Bristol, Tennessee   August 4, 1927

    39767-4   The Soldier's Sweetheart

BLUEBIRD 33-0513

    Own, vocal, yodel, guitar; Acc. The Three Southerners; Ellsworth T. Cozzens, steel guitar; Julian R. Ninde, guitar

    Camden, New Jersey   February 14, 1928

    41739-1   The Sailor's Plea

Victor 20864 "The Soldier's Sweetheart" only

Victor V-40054 "The Sailor's Plea" only

ELECTRADISK 78 RPM - Label Releases

Electradisk was a subsequent label that released Jimmie Rodger's original Victor record label recordings in the 1930's. You will find in this section each record's information and which original VICTOR record it was originally issued. With the exception of ELECTRADISK 2155 which shows the BLUEBIRD issue it was released on (This Bluebird issue was the first release of those Jimmie Rodger's tracks).

ELECTRADISK 1830

Acc. Lani McIntire's Hawaiian's; Sam Koki, steel guitar; Lani McIntire, guitar; unknown, ukulele; unknown, string bass;

Hollywood, California   June 30, 1930

54851-3   Moonlight And Skies

ELECTRADISK 1830

Acc. Clayton McMichen, fiddle; Oddie McWinders, banjo; Hoyt "Slim" Bryant, guitar;

Camden, New Jersey   August 11, 1932

58963-1A   Rock All Our Babies To Sleep

Victor 23574 "Moonlight And Skies" only

Victor 23721 "Rock All Our Babies To Sleep" only

ELECTRADISK 1958

Acc. Lani McIntire's Hawaiian's; Sam Koki, steel guitar; Lani McIntire, guitar; unknown, ukulele; unknown, string bass;

Hollywood, California   June 30, 1930

54851-3   Moonlight And Skies

ELECTRADISK 1958

Acc. Clayton McMichen, fiddle; Oddie McWinders, banjo; Hoyt "Slim" Bryant, guitar;

Camden, New Jersey   August 11, 1932

58963-1A   Rock All Our Babies To Sleep

Victor 23574 "Moonlight And Skies" only

Victor 23721 "Rock All Our Babies To Sleep" only

ELECTRADISK 1966

    Own, ukulele; Acc. Cliff Carlisle, steel guitar; Wilbur Ball, guitar;

    Louisville, Kentucky   June 15, 1931

    69443-3   Looking For A New Mama

ELECTRADISK 1966

    Acc. Clayton McMichen, fiddle; Oddie McWinders, banjo; Hoyt "Slim" Bryant, guitar;

    Camden, New Jersey   August 16, 1932

    58971-3   Gambling Barroom Blues

Victor 23580 "Looking For A New Mama" only

Victor 23766 "Gambling Barroom Blues" only

ELECTRADISK 1983

    Acc. Joe Kaipo, steel guitar; Billy Burkes, guitar; Weldon Burkes, ukulele

    Dallas, Texas   October 22, 1929

    56449-3   Whisper Your Mother's Name

ELECTRADISK 1983

    Own, vocal, guitar;

    Atlanta, Georgia   November 26, 1929

    56608-1   She Was Happy Till She Met You

Victor 22319 "Whisper Your Mother's Name" only

Victor 23681 "She Was Happy Till She Met You" only

ELECTRADISK 1999

    Acc. Clayton McMichen, fiddle; Oddie McWinders, banjo; Hoyt "Slim" Bryant, guitar;

    Camden, New Jersey   August 11, 1932

    58964-1   Whippin' That Old T.B.

ELECTRADISK 1999

    Acc. unknown, fiddle; unknown, fiddle; unknown, clarinet; unknown, piano; Hoyt "Slim" Bryant, guitar;

    New York City   August 29, 1932

    73325-1   Prairie Lullaby

Victor 23751 "Whippin' That Old T.B." only

Victor 23781 "Prairie Lullaby" only

ELECTRADISK 2008

Acc. Clayton McMichen, fiddle; Oddie McWinders, banjo; Hoyt "Slim" Bryant, guitar;

Camden, New Jersey August 11, 1932

58961-2A Mother, Queen Of My Heart

ELECTRADISK 2008

Acc. Clayton McMichen, fiddle; Oddie McWinders, banjo; Hoyt "Slim" Bryant, guitar;

Camden, New Jersey August 15, 1932

58970-2A Peach Pickin' Time Down In Georgia

Victor 23721 "Mother, Queen Of My Heart" only

Victor 23781 "Peach Pickin' Time Down In Georgia" only

ELECTRADISK 2009

Own, vocal, guitar;

Camden, New Jersey June 12, 1928

45094-1 You And My Old Guitar

ELECTRADISK 2009

Own, guitar; Acc. Billy Burkes, steel guitar; Weldon Burkes, guitar; Fred Koone, string bass;

Dallas, Texas February 4, 1932

70647-3 My Time Ain't Long

Victor 23669 "My Time Ain't Long" only

Victor V-40072 "You And My Old Guitar" only

ELECTRADISK 2042

Own, guitar; Acc. Billy Burkes, steel guitar; Weldon Burkes, guitar; Fred Koone, string bass;

Dallas, Texas February 4, 1932

45091-5 Mississippi Moon

ELECTRADISK 2042

    Own, guitar;

    New York CityMay 20, 1933

    76192-1Old Pal Of My Heart

Victor 23696 "Mississippi Moon" only

Victor 23816 "Old Pal Of My Heart" only

ELECTRADISK 2060

    Own, vocal, vocal effects; Acc. C.L. Hutchison, cornet; James Rikard, clarinet; John Westbrook, steel guitar; Dean Bryan, guitar; George MacMillan, string bass

    Atlanta, GeorgiaOctober 22, 1928

    47223-4Waiting For A Train

ELECTRADISK 2060

    Own, vocal, yodel; Acc. Cliff Carlisle, steel guitar; Wilbur Ball, guitar;

    Louisville, KentuckyJune 13, 1931

    69432-2When The Cactus Is In Bloom

Victor 23636 "When The Cactus Is In Bloom" only

Victor V-40014 "Waiting For A Train" only

ELECTRADISK 2109

    Own, vocal; Own, guitar; Ellsworth T. Cozzens, banjo

    Camden, New JerseyFebruary 15, 1928

    41740-1In The Jailhouse Now

ELECTRADISK 2109

    Own, vocal, guitar;

    Dallas, TexasAugust 10, 1929

    55333-2Frankie And Johnny

Victor 21245 "In The Jailhouse Now" only

Victor 22143 "Frankie And Johnny" only

ELECTRADISK 2155

    Own, guitar;

    New York City   May 18, 1933

    76160-1   Jimmie Rodgers' Last Blue Yodel

    Own, guitar;

    New York City   May 24, 1933

    76332-1   Years Ago

Bluebird B-5281

MONTGOMERY WARD 78 RPM - Label Releases

Montgomery Ward was a subsequent label that released Jimmie Rodger's original Victor record label recordings in the 1930's. You will find in this section each record's information and which original VICTOR record it was originally issued or in some cases BLUEBIRD record it was issued on. (Tracks showing the Bluebird label are tracks that were not released on the Victor label originally).

MONTGOMERY WARD 3272

    Own, vocal, yodel; Own, guitar

    Camden, New Jersey   November 30, 1927

    40753-2   Blue Yodel

    40754-2   Away Out On The Mountain

Victor 21142

MONTGOMERY WARD 4047

    Own, vocal; Acc. C.L. Hutchison, cornet; John Westbrook, steel guitar; Dean Bryan, guitar; George MacMillan, string bass

    Atlanta, Georgia   October 22, 1928

    47224-5   I'm Lonely And Blue

Rev. by Bud Billings

Victor V-40054

MONTGOMERY WARD 4058

    Own, guitar;

    Dallas, Texas   October 22, 1929

    56454-3   Yodeling Cowboy

Rev. by Bud Billings
Victor 22271

MONTGOMERY WARD 4067

    Own, vocal, yodel, guitar; Acc. Charles Kama, steel guitar

    San Antonio, Texas   January 31, 1931

    67133-3   T.B. Blues

Rev. by Gene Autry
Victor 23535

MONTGOMERY WARD 4200

    Acc. unknown, fiddle; unknown, fiddle; unknown, clarinet; unknown, piano; Hoyt "Slim" Bryant, guitar;

    New York City   August 29, 1932

    73324-1   In The Hills Of Tennessee

MONTGOMERY WARD 4200

    Acc. Clayton McMichen, fiddle; Oddie McWinders, banjo; Hoyt "Slim" Bryant, guitar;

    Camden, New Jersey   August 15, 1932

    58970-2A   Peach Pickin' Time Down In Georgia

Victor 23736 "In The Hills Of Tennessee" only
Victor 23781 "Peach Pickin' Time Down In Georgia" only

MONTGOMERY WARD 4201

    Acc. Clayton McMichen, fiddle; Oddie McWinders, banjo; Hoyt "Slim" Bryant, guitar;

    Camden, New Jersey   August 11, 1932

    58963-1A   Rock All Our Babies To Sleep

MONTGOMERY WARD 4201

    Acc. unknown, fiddle; unknown, fiddle; unknown, clarinet; unknown, piano; Hoyt "Slim" Bryant, guitar;

    New York City   August 29, 1932

    73325-1   Prairie Lullaby

Victor 23721 Rock All Our Babies To Sleep" only

Victor 23781 "Prairie Lullaby" only

MONTGOMERY WARD 4202

    Own, guitar; Acc. Fred Koone, guitar;

    Dallas, Texas   February 5, 1932

    70649-1   Down The Old Road To Home

MONTGOMERY WARD 4202

    Own, guitar; Acc. Oddie McWinders, banjo;

    Camden, New Jersey   August 15, 1932

    58969-1A   Long Tall Mamma Blues

Victor 23711 "Down The Old Road To Home" only

Victor 23766 "Long Tall Mamma Blues" only

MONTGOMERY WARD 4203

    Own, ukulele; Acc. Cliff Carlisle, steel guitar; Wilbur Ball, guitar;

    Louisville, Kentucky   June 15, 1931

    69443-3   Looking For A New Mama

MONTGOMERY WARD 4203

    Acc. Clayton McMichen, fiddle; Oddie McWinders, banjo; Hoyt "Slim" Bryant, guitar;

    Camden, New Jersey   August 16, 1932

    58971-3   Gambling Barroom Blues

Victor 23580 "Looking For A New Mama" only

Victor 23766 "Gambling Barroom Blues" only

MONTGOMERY WARD 4204

Own, vocal, yodel; Acc. Lani McIntire's Hawaiian's; Sam Koki, steel guitar; Lani McIntire, guitar; unknown, ukulele; unknown, string bass;

Hollywood, California   June 30, 1930

54850-3   Why Should I Be Lonely

MONTGOMERY WARD 4204

Acc. Clayton McMichen, fiddle; Oddie McWinders, banjo; Hoyt "Slim" Bryant, guitar;

Camden, New Jersey   August 11, 1932

58964-1   Whippin' That Old T.B.

Victor 23609 "Why Should I Be Lonely" only

Victor 23751 "Whippin' That Old T.B." only

MONTGOMERY WARD 4205

Acc. Dick Bunyard, steel guitar; Red Young, mandolin; Bill Boyd, guitar; Fred Koone, string bass;

Dallas, Texas   February 3, 1932

70646-1   Hobo's Meditation

MONTGOMERY WARD 4205

Own, guitar; Acc. Clayton McMichen, fiddle; Hoyt "Slim" Bryant, guitar;

Camden, New Jersey   August 15, 1932

58968-2A   No Hard Times

Victor 23711 "Hobo's Meditation" only

Victor 23751 "No Hard Times" only

MONTGOMERY WARD 4206

Acc. Clayton McMichen, fiddle; Oddie McWinders, banjo; Hoyt "Slim" Bryant, guitar;

Camden, New Jersey   August 11, 1932

58961-2A   Mother, Queen Of My Heart

MONTGOMERY WARD 4206

Acc. unknown, fiddle; unknown, fiddle; unknown, clarinet; unknown, piano; Hoyt "Slim" Bryant, guitar;

New York City   August 29, 1932

73326-1   Miss The Mississippi And You

Victor 23721 "Mother, Queen Of My Heart" only

Victor 23736 "Miss The Mississippi And You" only

MONTGOMERY WARD 4207

Acc. Joe Kaipo, steel guitar; Billy Burkes, guitar; Weldon Burkes, ukulele

Dallas, Texas   October 22, 1929

56449-3   Whisper Your Mother's Name

MONTGOMERY WARD 4207

Own, vocal, guitar;

Atlanta, Georgia   November 26, 1929

56608-1   She Was Happy Till She Met You

Victor 22319 "Whisper Your Mother's Name" only

Victor 23681 "She Was Happy Till She Met You" only

MONTGOMERY WARD 4208

Acc. Ruth Ann Moore, piano;

Louisville, Kentucky   June 16, 1931

69448-1   What's It?

MONTGOMERY WARD 4208

Own, guitar;

Dallas, Texas   February 6, 1932

70650-1 Blue Yodel No. 10 (Ground Hog Rootin' In My Back Yard)

Victor 23609 "What's It?" only

Victor 23696 "Blue Yodel No. 10 (Ground Hog Rootin' In My Back Yard)" only

MONTGOMERY WARD 4209

    Acc. Louis Armstrong, trumpet; Lillian Hardin Armstrong, piano;

    Hollywood, California   July 16, 1930

    54867-2   Blue Yodel No. 9

MONTGOMERY WARD 4209

    Own, vocal, yodel, guitar;

    Louisville, Kentucky   July 11, 1931

    69424-3   Let Me Be Your Side Track

Victor 23580 "Blue Yodel No. 9" only

Victor 23621 "Let Me Be Your Side Track" only

MONTGOMERY WARD 4210

    Own, vocal, vocal effects; Acc. Billy Burkes, guitar;

    New Orleans, Louisiana or Atlanta, Georgia (Unclear Where Session Was Recorded)   November 13, 1929

    56528-1   Hobo Bill's Last Ride

MONTGOMERY WARD 4210

    Own, vocal, guitar; Acc. Billy Burkes, guitar

    Atlanta, Georgia   November 26, 1929

    56607-1   Anniversary Blue Yodel (Blue Yodel No. 7)

Victor 22421 "Hobo Bill's Last Ride" only

Victor 22488 "Anniversary Blue Yodel (Blue Yodel No. 7)" only

MONTGOMERY WARD 4211

    Own, guitar;

    Dallas, Texas   October 22, 1929

    56453-2   Blue Yodel No. 6

MONTGOMERY WARD 4211

    Acc. Lani McIntire, guitar;

    Hollywood, California   July 5, 1930

    54855-1   Those Gambler's Blues

Victor 22271 "Blue Yodel No. 6" only

Victor 22554 "Those Gambler's Blues" only

MONTGOMERY WARD 4212

    Own, vocal, guitar;

    New York City   February 23, 1929

    49990-2   Blue Yodel No. 5

MONTGOMERY WARD 4212

    Own, vocal, guitar; Acc. Joe Kaipo, steel guitar; Billy Burkes, guitar;

    Dallas, Texas   August 10, 1929

    55332-2   Jimmie's Texas Blues

Victor 22072 "Blue Yodel No. 5" only

Victor 22379 "Jimmie's Texas Blues" only

MONTGOMERY WARD 4213

    Own, vocal, guitar;

    Camden, New Jersey   February 15, 1928

    41743-2   Blue Yodel No. 3

MONTGOMERY WARD 4213

    Own, guitar;

    Dallas, Texas   October 22, 1929

    56454-3   Yodeling Cowboy

Victor 21531 "Blue Yodel No. 3" only

Victor 22271 "Yodeling Cowboy" only

MONTGOMERY WARD 4214

    Own, vocal, yodel, guitar; Acc. The Three Southerners; Ellsworth T. Cozzens, ukulele

    Camden, New Jersey   February 14, 1928

    41738-1   The Brakeman's Blues (Yodeling The Blues Away)

MONTGOMERY WARD 4214

    Own, vocal, guitar; Acc. Ellsworth T. Cozzens, steel guitar

    Camden, New Jersey   February 15, 1928

    41741-2   Blue Yodel – No. II (My Lovin' Gal Lucille)

Victor 21291

MONTGOMERY WARD 4215

Own, vocal, guitar; Acc. Joe Kaipo, steel guitar;

Dallas, Texas October 22, 1929

56455-1 My Rough And Rowdy Ways

MONTGOMERY WARD 4215

Own, guitar, vocal effects; Acc. Billy Burkes, guitar; Weldon Burkes, guitar; Fred Koone, string bass; Charlie Burkes, ukulele;

Dallas, Texas February 4, 1932

70648-2 Ninety Nine Years Blues

Victor 2220 "My Rough And Rowdy Ways" only

Victor 23669 "Ninety Nine Years Blues" only

MONTGOMERY WARD 4216

Acc. Lani McIntire's Hawaiian's; Sam Koki, steel guitar; Lani McIntire, guitar; unknown, ukulele; unknown, string bass;

Hollywood, California June 30, 1930

54851-3 Moonlight And Skies

MONTGOMERY WARD 4216

Own, vocal, yodel; Acc. Cliff Carlisle, steel guitar; Wilbur Ball, guitar;

Louisville, Kentucky June 13, 1931

69432-2 When The Cactus Is In Bloom

Victor 23574 "Moonlight And Skies" only

Victor 23636 "When The Cactus Is In Bloom" only

MONTGOMERY WARD 4217

Own, vocal, yodel; Acc. The Three Southerners; Ellsworth T. Cozzens, steel guitar; Julian R. Ninde, guitar

Camden, New Jersey February 14, 1928

41737 Treasures Untold

MONTGOMERY WARD 4217

Own, vocal; Acc. C.L. Hutchison, cornet; John Westbrook, steel guitar; Dean Bryan, guitar; George MacMillan, string bass

Atlanta, Georgia   October 22, 1928

47224-5   I'm Lonely And Blue

Victor 21433 "Treasures Untold" only
Victor V-40054 "I'm Lonely And Blue" only

MONTGOMERY WARD 4218

Own, vocal, yodel, guitar

Camden, New Jersey   June 12, 1928

45093-1   My Little Old Home Down In New Orleans

MONTGOMERY WARD 4218

Own, vocal, guitar;

Camden, New Jersey   June 12, 1928

45098-2   Lullaby Yodel

Victor 21574 "My Little Old Home Down In New Orleans" only
Victor 21636 "Lullaby Yodel" only

MONTGOMERY WARD 4219

Own, vocal, yodel; Acc. Dick Bunyard, steel guitar; Red Young, mandolin; Bill Boyd, guitar' Fred Koone, string bass;

Dallas, Texas   February 2, 1932

70645-2   Roll Along Kentucky Moon

MONTGOMERY WARD 4219

Own, guitar; Acc. Joe Kaipo, steel guitar;

Dallas, Texas   August 12, 1929

55345-4   Home Call

Victor 23651 "Roll Along Kentucky Moon" only
Victor 23681 "Home Call" only

MONTGOMERY WARD 4220

Own, vocal; Acc. Lani McIntire's Hawaiian's; Sam Koki, steel guitar; Lani McIntire, guitar; unknown, ukulele; unknown, string bass;

Hollywood, California   July 7, 1930

54856-2   I'm Lonesome Too

MONTGOMERY WARD 4220

Own, guitar; Acc. Billy Burkes, steel guitar; Weldon Burkes, guitar; Fred Koone, string bass;

Dallas, Texas   February 4, 1932

45091-5   Mississippi Moon

Victor 23564 "I'm Lonesome Too" only

Victor 23696 "Mississippi Moon" only

MONTGOMERY WARD 4221

Acc. Joe Kaipo, steel guitar; Billy Burkes, guitar; Weldon Burkes, ukulele

Atlanta, Georgia   November 28, 1929

56618-1   A Drunkard's Child

MONTGOMERY WARD 4221

Own, vocal, yodel; Acc. Lani McIntire's Hawaiian's; Sam Koki, steel guitar; Lani McIntire, guitar; unknown, ukulele; unknown, string bass;

Hollywood, California   July 9, 1930

54860-3   For The Sake Of Days Gone By

Victor 22319 "A Drunkard's Child" only

Victor 23651 "For The Sake Of Days Gone By" only

MONTGOMERY WARD 4222

Acc. Billy Burkes, guitar;

Atlanta, Georgia   November 28, 1929

56619-1   That's Why I'm Blue

MONTGOMERY WARD 4222

    Acc. Bob Sawyer's Jazz Band; unknown, cornet; unknown, clarinet; Bob Sawyer, piano; unknown, banjo; unknown, tuba;

    Hollywood, California   June 30, 1930

    54849-2   My Blue Eyed Jane

Victor 22421 "That's Why I'm Blue" only

Victor 23549 "My Blue Eyed Jane" only

MONTGOMERY WARD 4223

    Own, vocal, guitar; Acc. Joe Kaipo, steel guitar; Billy Burkes, guitar; Weldon Burkes, Ukulele; Bob MacGimsey, whistle

    Dallas, Texas   August 8, 1929

    55309-2   Train Whistle Blues

MONTGOMERY WARD 4223

    Own, vocal, guitar, effects

    Hollywood, California   July 11, 1930

    54862-3   The Mystery Of Number Five

Victor 22379 "Train Whistle Blues" only

Victor 23549 "The Mystery Of Number Five" only

MONTGOMERY WARD 4224

    Own, vocal; Own, guitar

    Camden, New Jersey   November 30, 1927

    40752   My Mother Was A Lady

MONTGOMERY WARD 4224

    Own, vocal, guitar;

    Camden, New Jersey   June 12, 1928

    45094-1   You And My Old Guitar

Victor 21433 "My Mother Was A Lady" only

Victor V-40072 "You And My Old Guitar" only

MONTGOMERY WARD 4309

    Own, vocal, guitar;
    Dallas, Texas   August 10, 1929
    55333-2   Frankie And Johnny

Rev. by Leonard Stokes
Victor 22143

MONTGOMERY WARD 4315

    Own, vocal, guitar;
    Hollywood, California   July 12, 1930
    54864-1   In The Jail-House Now – No. 2

Rev. by Jimmy Long
Victor 22523

MONTGOMERY WARD 4316

    Own, vocal, yodel, guitar;
    Hollywood, California   July 1, 1930
    54852-2   Pistol Packin' Papa

Rev. by Jimmy Long
Victor 22523

MONTGOMERY WARD 4324

    Own, vocal, guitar;
    Atlanta, Georgia   November 26, 1929
    56608-1   She Was Happy Till She Met You

Rev. by Harry McClintock
❖ Some issues titled as "She's More To Be Pitied Than Censured"
Victor 23681 "She Was Happy Till She Met You" only

MONTGOMERY WARD 4415

    Own, guitar;
    New York City   May 18, 1933
    76160-1   Jimmie Rodgers' Last Blue Yodel

MONTGOMERY WARD 4415

Own, guitar;

New York City May 24, 1933

76332-1 Years Ago

Bluebird B-5281

MONTGOMERY WARD 4450

Own, vocal, guitar; Acc. Ellsworth T. Cozzens, steel guitar

Camden, New Jersey February 15, 1928

41742-2 Memphis Yodel

MONTGOMERY WARD 4450

Own, guitar;

Dallas, Texas October 22, 1929

56450-1 The Land Of My Boyhood Dreams

Victor 21636"Memphis Yodel" only

Victor 23811 "The Land Of My Boyhood Dreams" only

MONTGOMERY WARD 4451

Own, vocal; Acc. C.L. Hutchison, cornet; James Rikard, clarinet; John Westbrook, steel guitar; Dean Bryan, guitar; George MacMillan, string bass

Atlanta, Georgia October 20, 1928

47215-3 My Carolina Sunshine Girl

MONTGOMERY WARD 4451

Own, vocal; Acc. unknown, violin; unknown, clarinet; unknown, cornet; unknown, piano; unknown, tuba; unknown, traps;

New York City February 21, 1929

48384-3 Desert Blues

Victor V-40096

MONTGOMERY WARD 4452
    Own, vocal; Own, guitar
    Bristol, Tennessee August 4, 1927
    39767-4 The Soldier's Sweetheart
    39768-3 Sleep, Baby, Sleep
Victor 20864

MONTGOMERY WARD 4453
    Own, guitar;
    New York City May 17, 1933
    76141-1 I'm Free (From The Chain Gang Now)

MONTGOMERY WARD 4453
    Own, guitar;
    New York City May 20, 1933
    76191-1 The Yodeling Ranger
Victor 23830

MONTGOMERY WARD 4454
    Acc. John Cali, steel guitar; Tony Colicchio, guitar;
    New York City May 24, 1933
    76327-1 Old Love Letters (Bring Memories Of You)

MONTGOMERY WARD 4454
    Acc. John Cali, guitar; Tony Colicchio, guitar;
    New York City May 24, 1933
    76331-1 Somewhere Down Below The Dixon Line
Victor 23840

MONTGOMERY WARD 4720
    Acc. Lani McIntire's Hawaiian's; Sam Koki, steel guitar; Lani McIntire, guitar; unknown, ukulele; unknown, string bass;
    Hollywood, California June 30, 1930
    54851-3 Moonlight And Skies

MONTGOMERY WARD 4720

Own, vocal, yodel, speaking; Sara Carters, vocal, speaking, guitar; A.P. Carter, vocal, speaking; Maybelle Carter, vocal, speaking, mandolin, guitar;

Louisville, Kentucky   June 12, 1931
69427-4   Jimmie Rodgers Visits The Carter Family

Victor 23574

MONTGOMERY WARD 4721

Own, vocal; Own, guitar; Ellsworth T. Cozzens, banjo

Camden, New Jersey   February 15, 1928
41740-1   In The Jailhouse Now

MONTGOMERY WARD 4721

Own, vocal, guitar;

Dallas, Texas   August 10, 1929
55333-2   Frankie And Johnny

Victor 21245 "In The Jailhouse Now" only

Victor 22143 "Frankie And Johnny" only

MONTGOMERY WARD 4722

Acc. Billy Burkes, guitar

Atlanta, Georgia   November 25, 1929
56594-3   Mississippi River Blues

MONTGOMERY WARD 4722

Own, vocal; Acc. C.L. Hutchison, cornet; James Rikard, clarinet; John Westbrook, steel guitar; Dean Bryan, guitar; George MacMillan, string bass

Atlanta, Georgia   October 20, 1928
47216-4   Blue Yodel No. 4 (California Blues)

Victor 23535 "Mississippi River Blues" only

Victor V-40014 "Blue Yodel No. 4 (California Blues)" only

MONTGOMERY WARD 4723

Acc. Bob Sawyer's Jazz Band; unknown, cornet; unknown, clarinet; Bob Sawyer, piano; unknown, banjo; unknown, tuba;

Hollywood, California   July 10, 1930

54861-3   Jimmie's Mean Mama Blues

MONTGOMERY WARD 4723

Own, guitar; Acc. Bob Sawyer's Jazz Band; unknown, cornet; unknown, clarinet; Bob Sawyer, piano; unknown, banjo; unknown, tuba;

Hollywood, California   July 11, 1930

54863-1   Blue Yodel No. 8 (Mule Skinner Blues)

Victor 23503

MONTGOMERY WARD 4724

Own, vocal, guitar;

Hollywood, California   July 12, 1930

54864-1   In The Jail-House Now – No. 2

MONTGOMERY WARD 4724

Acc. Billy Burkes, guitar

Atlanta, Georgia   November 25, 1929

56595-4   Nobody Knows But Me

Victor 22523 "In The Jail-House Now – No. 2" only

Victor 23518 "Nobody Knows But Me" only

MONTGOMERY WARD 4725

Own, vocal, guitar; Acc. Ellsworth T. Cozzens, steel guitar

Camden, New Jersey   February 15, 1928

41742-2   Memphis Yodel

MONTGOMERY WARD 4725

Own, guitar;

Dallas, Texas   February 6, 1932

70650-1 Blue Yodel No. 10 (Ground Hog Rootin' In My Back Yard)

Victor 21636 "Memphis Yodel" only

Victor 23696 "Blue Yodel No. 10 (Ground Hog Rootin' In My Back Yard)" only

MONTGOMERY WARD 4726

    Own, vocal, guitar; Billy Burkes, guitar

    Atlanta, Georgia   November 27, 1929

    56617-1   Blue Yodel Number Eleven

MONTGOMERY WARD 4726

    Acc. Hoyt "Slim" Bryant, guitar; unknown, fiddle; unknown, fiddle; unknown, clarinet; unknown, piano;

    New York City   August 29, 1932

    73327-1   Sweet Mama Hurry Home Or I'll Be Gone

Victor 23796

MONTGOMERY WARD 4727

    Own, guitar;

    New York City   May 17, 1933

    76138-1   Blue Yodel No. 12

    76140-1   The Cow Hand's Last Ride

Victor 24456

MONTGOMERY WARD 4728

    Own, guitar;

    Dallas, Texas   October 22, 1929

    56450-1   The Land Of My Boyhood Dreams

MONTGOMERY WARD 4728

    Own, guitar;

    Louisville, Kentucky   June 16, 1931

    69458-1   Southern Cannon-Ball

Victor 23811

MONTGOMERY WARD 4729

Own, vocal, yodel, guitar; Acc. Charles Kama, steel guitar

San Antonio, Texas   January 31, 1931

67133-3   T.B. Blues

MONTGOMERY WARD 4729

Acc. Shelly Lee Alley, fiddle; Alvin Alley, fiddle; Charles Kama, steel guitar; M.T. Salazar, guitar; Mike Cordova, string bass;

San Antonio, Texas   January 31, 1931

67134-2   Travellin' Blues

Victor 23535 "T.B. Blues" only

Victor 23564 "Travellin' Blues" only

MONTGOMERY WARD 4730

Own, vocal, guitar; Acc. unknown, violin; unknown, clarinet; unknown, cornet; unknown, piano; unknown, tuba; unknown, traps;

New York City   February 21, 1929

48385-1   Any Old Time

MONTGOMERY WARD 4730

Own, vocal, yodel, guitar;

Hollywood, California   July 1, 1930

54852-2   Pistol Packin' Papa

Victor 22488 "Any Old Time" only

Victor 22554 "Pistol Packin' Papa" only

MONTGOMERY WARD 4731

Acc. Charles Kama, steel guitar; M.T. Salazar, guitar; Mike Cordova, string bass;

San Antonio, Texas   January 31, 1931

67135-1   Jimmie The Kid (Parts Of The Life Of Rodgers)

MONTGOMERY WARD 4731

Own, vocal, guitar;

Camden, New Jersey   June 12, 1928

45096-1   My Little Lady

Victor 23549 "Jimmie The Kid (Parts Of The Life Of Rodgers)" only
Victor V-40072 "My Little Lady" only

MONTGOMERY WARD 5013
    Own, vocal, guitar;
    Dallas, Texas   October 22, 1929
    56456-3   I've Ranged, I've Roamed, I've Travelled

MONTGOMERY WARD 5013
    Acc. Billy Burkes, guitar;
    Atlanta, Georgia   November 28, 1929
    56620-3   Why Did You Give Me Your Love?

Bluebird B-5892

MONTGOMERY WARD 5014
    Acc. The Louisville Jug Band; Clifford Hayes, fiddle; George Allen, clarinet; Cal Smith, guitar; Freddie Smith, guitar; Earl McDonald, jug;
    Louisville, Kentucky   June 16, 1931
    69499-3   My Good Gal's Gone – Blues

Rev. by Jesse Rodgers
Bluebird B-5942

MONTGOMERY WARD 5036
    Own, vocal, guitar; Acc. Joe Kaipo, steel guitar; Billy Burkes, guitar; Weldon Burkes, Ukulele; Bob MacGimsey, whistle
    Dallas, Texas   August 8, 1929
    55308-1   Tuck Away My Lonesome Blues

MONTGOMERY WARD 5036
    Own, vocal, yodel, guitar; Acc. The Three Southerners; Ellsworth T. Cozzens, steel guitar; Julian R. Ninde, guitar
    Camden, New Jersey   February 14, 1928
    41739-1   The Sailor's Plea

Victor 22220 "Tuck Away My Lonesome Blues" only
Victor V-40054 "The Sailor's Plea" only

MONTGOMERY WARD 7137

Own, vocal, yodel, speaking; Sara Carters, vocal, speaking, guitar; A.P. Carter, vocal, speaking; Maybelle Carter, vocal, speaking, mandolin, guitar;

Louisville, Kentucky					June 11, 1931

69428-4			The Carter Family And Jimmie Rodgers In Texas

MONTGOMERY WARD 7137 (as by Jimmie Rodgers-Sara Carter)

Vocal, yodel duet; Acc. Sara Carter, guitar; Maybelle Carter, guitar;

Louisville, Kentucky					June 10, 1931

69413-2						The Wonderful City

Bluebird B-6762 "The Carter Family And Jimmie Rodgers In Texas" only

Bluebird B-6810 "The Wonderful City" only

MONTGOMERY WARD 7138

Vocal, yodel duet; Acc. Maybelle Carter, guitar;

Louisville, Kentucky					June 10, 1931

69412-1					Why There's A Tear In My Eye

MONTGOMERY WARD 7138

Acc. Clayton McMichen, fiddle; Oddie McWinders, banjo; Hoyt "Slim" Bryant, guitar;

Camden, New Jersey					August 16, 1932

58972-1					I've Only Loved Three Women

Bluebird B-6698 "Why There's A Tear In My Eye" only

Bluebird B-6810 "I've Only Loved Three Women" only

MONTGOMERY WARD 7139

Own, guitar;

New York City						May 18, 1933

76151-1					Yodeling My Way Back Home

MONTGOMERY WARD 7139

Own, guitar;

New York City						May 17, 1933

76139-1					Dreaming With Tears In My Eyes

Bluebird B-7280 " Yodeling My Way Back Home" only

Bluebird B-7600 "Dreaming With Tears In My Eyes" only

MONTGOMERY WARD 8109

Own, vocal, guitar;

Camden, New Jersey — June 12, 1928

45090-1 — My Old Pal

45095-1 — Daddy And Home

MONTGOMERY WARD 8109

Own, vocal, vocal effects; Acc. C.L. Hutchison, cornet; James Rikard, clarinet; John Westbrook, steel guitar; Dean Bryan, guitar; George MacMillan, string bass

Atlanta, Georgia — October 22, 1928

47223-4 — Waiting For A Train

Victor 21757 "Daddy And Home" only

Victor V-40014 "Waiting For A Train" only

MONTGOMERY WARD 8121

Own, vocal, guitar; Acc. Ellsworth T. Cozzens, steel guitar

Camden, New Jersey — February 15, 1928

41741-2 — Blue Yodel – No. II (My Lovin' Gal Lucille)

Rev. by Harry McClintock

Victor 21291

MONTGOMERY WARD 8124

Own, vocal; Acc. C.L. Hutchison, cornet; James Rikard, clarinet; John Westbrook, steel guitar; Dean Bryan, guitar; George MacMillan, string bass

Atlanta, Georgia — October 20, 1928

47216-4 — Blue Yodel No. 4 (California Blues)

Rev. by Bud And Joe Billings

Victor V-40014

MONTGOMERY WARD 8235

>Own, guitar; Acc. Bob Sawyer's Jazz Band; unknown, cornet; unknown, clarinet; Bob Sawyer, piano; unknown, banjo; unknown, tuba;
>
>Hollywood, California   July 11, 1930
>
>54863-1   Blue Yodel No. 8 (Mule Skinner Blues)

Rev. by Gene Autry

Victor 23503

SUNRISE 78 RPM - Label Releases

Sunrise was a subsequent label that released Jimmie Rodger's original Victor record label recordings in the 1930's. You will find in this section each record's information and which original VICTOR record it was originally issued.. With the exception of Sunrise 3362 which shows the BLUEBIRD issue it was released on (This Bluebird issue was the first release of those Jimmie Rodger's tracks).

SUNRISE 3104

>Acc. Lani McIntire's Hawaiian's; Sam Koki, steel guitar; Lani McIntire, guitar; unknown, ukulele; unknown, string bass;
>
>Hollywood, California   June 30, 1930
>
>54851-3   Moonlight And Skies

SUNRISE 3104

>Acc. Clayton McMichen, fiddle; Oddie McWinders, banjo; Hoyt "Slim" Bryant, guitar;
>
>Camden, New Jersey   August 11, 1932
>
>58963-1A   Rock All Our Babies To Sleep

Victor 23574 "Moonlight And Skies" only

Victor 23721 "Rock All Our Babies To Sleep" only

SUNRISE 3131

>Own, ukulele; Acc. Cliff Carlisle, steel guitar; Wilbur Ball, guitar;
>
>Louisville, Kentucky   June 15, 1931
>
>69443-3   Looking For A New Mama

SUNRISE 3131

    Acc. Clayton McMichen, fiddle; Oddie McWinders, banjo; Hoyt "Slim" Bryant, guitar;

    Camden, New Jersey   August 16, 1932

    58971-3   Gambling Barroom Blues

Victor 23580 "Looking For A New Mama" only

Victor 23766 "Gambling Barroom Blues" only

SUNRISE 3142

    Acc. Joe Kaipo, steel guitar; Billy Burkes, guitar; Weldon Burkes, ukulele

    Dallas, Texas   October 22, 1929

    56449-3   Whisper Your Mother's Name

SUNRISE 3142

    Own, vocal, guitar;

    Atlanta, Georgia   November 26, 1929

    56608-1   She Was Happy Till She Met You

Victor 22319 "Whisper Your Mother's Name" only

Victor 23681 "She Was Happy Till She Met You" only

SUNRISE 3157

    Acc. Clayton McMichen, fiddle; Oddie McWinders, banjo; Hoyt "Slim" Bryant, guitar;

    Camden, New Jersey   August 11, 1932

    58964-1   Whippin' That Old T.B

SUNRISE 3157

    Acc. unknown, fiddle; unknown, fiddle; unknown, clarinet; unknown, piano; Hoyt "Slim" Bryant, guitar;

    New York City   August 29, 1932

    73325-1   Prairie Lullaby

Victor 23751 "Whippin' That Old T.B." only

Victor 23781 "Prairie Lullaby" only

SUNRISE 3167

Acc. Clayton McMichen, fiddle; Oddie McWinders, banjo; Hoyt "Slim" Bryant, guitar;

Camden, New Jersey   August 11, 1932

58961-2A   Mother, Queen Of My Heart

SUNRISE 3167

Acc. Clayton McMichen, fiddle; Oddie McWinders, banjo; Hoyt "Slim" Bryant, guitar;

Camden, New Jersey   August 15, 1932

58970-2A   Peach Pickin' Time Down In Georgia

Victor 23721 "Mother, Queen Of My Heart" only

Victor 23781 "Peach Pickin' Time Down In Georgia" only

SUNRISE 3168

Own, guitar; Acc. Fred Koone, guitar;

Dallas, Texas   February 5, 1932

70649-1   Down The Old Road To Home

SUNRISE 3168

Acc. unknown, fiddle; unknown, fiddle; unknown, clarinet; unknown, piano; Hoyt "Slim" Bryant, guitar;

New York City   August 29, 1932

73326-1   Miss The Mississippi And You

Victor 23711 "Down The Old Road To Home" only

Victor 23736 "Miss The Mississippi And You" only

SUNRISE 3169

Own, vocal, yodel; Acc. Lani McIntire's Hawaiian's; Sam Koki, steel guitar; Lani McIntire, guitar; unknown, ukulele; unknown, string bass;

Hollywood, California   June 30, 1930

54850-3   Why Should I Be Lonely

SUNRISE 3169

    Own, vocal, yodel; Acc. Dick Bunyard, steel guitar; Red Young, mandolin; Bill Boyd, guitar' Fred Koone, string bass;

    Dallas, Texas   February 2, 1932

    70645-2   Roll Along Kentucky Moon

Victor 23609 "Why Should I Be Lonely" only

Victor 23651 "Roll Along Kentucky Moon" only

SUNRISE 3170

    Own, guitar; Acc. Billy Burkes, steel guitar; Weldon Burkes, guitar; Fred Koone, string bass;

    Dallas, Texas   February 4, 1932

    70647-3   My Time Ain't Long

SUNRISE 3170

    Own, vocal, guitar;

    Camden, New Jersey   June 12, 1928

    45094-1   You And My Old Guitar

Victor 23669 "My Time Ain't Long" only

Victor V-40072 "You And My Old Guitar" only

SUNRISE 3171

    Acc. Ruth Ann Moore, piano;

    Louisville, Kentucky   June 16, 1931

    69448-1   What's It?

SUNRISE 3171

    Own, vocal, yodel, guitar;

    Louisville, Kentucky   July 11, 1931

    69424-3   Let Me Be Your Side Track

Victor 23609 "What's It?" only

Victor 23621 "Let Me Be Your Side Track" only

SUNRISE 3172

Own, vocal, yodel; Own, guitar

Camden, New Jersey   November 30, 1927

40753-2   Blue Yodel

40754-2   Away Out On The Mountain

Victor 21142

SUNRISE 3217

Own, guitar; Acc. Billy Burkes, steel guitar; Weldon Burkes, guitar; Fred Koone, string bass;

Dallas, Texas   February 4, 1932

45091-5   Mississippi Moon

SUNRISE 3217

Own, guitar;

New York City   May 20, 1933

76192-1   Old Pal Of My Heart

Victor 23696 "Mississippi Moon" only

Victor 23811 "Old Pal Of My Heart" only

SUNRISE 3244

Own, vocal, yodel; Acc. Cliff Carlisle, steel guitar; Wilbur Ball, guitar;

Louisville, Kentucky   June 13, 1931

69432-2   When The Cactus Is In Bloom

SUNRISE 3244

Own, vocal, vocal effects; Acc. C.L. Hutchison, cornet; James Rikard, clarinet; John Westbrook, steel guitar; Dean Bryan, guitar; George MacMillan, string bass

Atlanta, Georgia   October 22, 1928

47223-4   Waiting For A Train

Victor 23636 "When The Cactus Is In Bloom" only

Victor V-40014 "Waiting For A Train" only

SUNRISE 3306

    Own, vocal; Own, guitar; Ellsworth T. Cozzens, banjo

    Camden, New Jersey   February 15, 1928

    41740-1   In The Jailhouse Now

SUNRISE 3306

    Own, vocal, guitar;

    Dallas, Texas   August 10, 1929

    55333-2   Frankie And Johnny

Victor 21245 "In The Jailhouse Now" only

Victor 22143 "Frankie And Johnny" only

SUNRISE 3362

    Own, guitar;

    New York City   May 18, 1933

    76160-1   Jimmie Rodgers' Last Blue Yodel

SUNRISE 3362

    Own, guitar;

    New York City   May 24, 1933

    76332-1   Years Ago

Bluebird B-5281

SUNRISE 3418

    Own, vocal, guitar;

    Camden, New Jersey   June 12, 1928

    45098-2   Lullaby Yodel

SUNRISE 3418

    Own, guitar;

    Dallas, Texas   October 22, 1929

    56450-1   The Land Of My Boyhood Dreams

Victor 21636 "Lullaby Yodel" only

Victor 23811 "The Land Of My Boyhood Dreams" only

Victor 21142-A Blue Yodel

Victor 21245-A Ben Dewberry's Final Run

Victor 21245-B In The Jailhouse Now

Victor 21433-A Treasures Untold

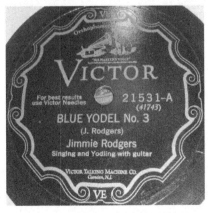
Victor 21531-A Blue Yodel No. 3

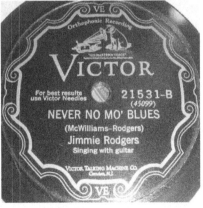
Victor 21531-B Never No Mo' Blues

Victor 21574-A My Little Old Home Down In New Orleans

Victor 21574-B Dear Old Sunny South By The Sea

Victor 21757-A My Old Pal

Victor 21757-B Daddy And Home

Victor 22072-A Blue Yodel No. 5

Victor 222271 –A Blue Yodel No. 6

Victor 22379-A Train Whistle Blues

Victor 22523-A High Powered Mama

Victor 22523-B In The Jail-House Now No. 2

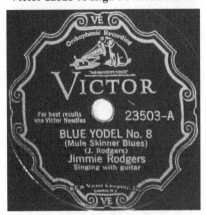

Victor 23503-A Blue Yodel No. 8

Victor 23518-A Nobody Knows But Me

Victor 23549-A Jimmie The Kid

Victor 23564-B I'm Lonesome Too

Victor 23574-A Jimmie Rodgers Visits The Carter Family

Victor 23580-A Blue Yodel Number 9

Victor 23609-A What's it?

Victor 23636-A Gambling Polka Dot Blues

Victor 23669-A Ninety Nine Years Blues

Victor V-40014-B Waiting For A Train

Victor V-40054-A I'm Lonely And Blue

Victor V-40072-A My Little Lady

RCA Victor 18-6000-A Cowboy's Last Ride

RCA Victor 18-6000-B Blue Yodel No. 12 (Picture shows all 12 Yodel Songs)

89

Bluebird B-5000 Moonlight And Skies   Bluebird B-5136 Mississippi Moon

Bluebird B-5163 When The Cactus Is In Bloom   Bluebird B-5223 In The Jailhouse Now

Bluebird B-5281 Jimmie Rodger's Last Blue Yodel   Bluebird B-5393 Mississippi River Blues

Bluebird B-5556 My Carolina Sunshine Girl

Bluebird B-5942 My Good Gal's Gone Blues

Bluebird B-6762 The Carter Family & Jimmie Rodgers In Texas

Bluebird B-6810 The Wonderful City

Bluebird B-7280-A The One Rose

Bluebird B-7280-B Yodeling My Way Back Home

Bluebird B-7600 Take Me Back Again

MW M-3272-A Blue Yodel

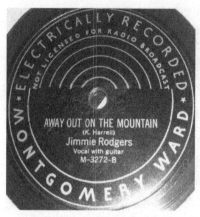

MW M-3272-B Away On The Mountain

MW M-4200 Peach Picking Time In Georgia

MW M-4200-B In The Hills Of Tennessee

MW M-4204-A Whippin' That Old T. B.

MW M-4204-B Why Should I Be Lonely?

MW M-4210-B Hobo Bill's Last Ride

MW M-4212-B Jimmie's Texas Blues

MW M-4215-A Ninety Nine Years Blues

MW M-4219-A Roll Along Kentucky Moon

MW M-4219-B Home Call

MW M-4454-A Old Love Letters MW M-4726-A Blue Yodel No. 11

MW M-4727-A Blue Yodel No. 12 MW M-4729 Travellin' Blues

MW M-5013-A I've Ranged, I've Roamed And I've Traveled

(UK) Regal Zonophone MR 2700
Yodelling My Way Back Home

(UK) Regal Zonophone MR 3122
Blue Yodel No. 2

(UK) Regal Zonophone T5341 My Little Old Home Town In New Orleans

(UK) Regal Zonophone T5577 Everybody Does It In Hawaii

(UK) Zonophone 5158 Blue Yodel

(UK) Zonophone 5247 Never No Mo' Blues

95

(UK) Zonophone 5283 Memphis Yodel

(UK) Zonophone 5423 You And My Old Guitar

(UK) Zonophone 5983 Tuck Away My Lonesome Blues

(Australian) Regal-Zonophone EE345 Gambling Polka Dot Blues

(Australian) Regal-Zonophone G23189 Mississippi Moon

RCA Victor (Promotional) 47-6092
In The Jailhouse Now No. 2

RCA Victor (Promotional) 47-6408
Daddy And Home

RCA Victor EPA-21 Yodelingly Yours
Vol. 1 (Blue Sleeve)

RCA Victor EPA-22 Yodelingly Yours
Vol. 2 (Orange Sleeve)

RCA Victor EPA-23 Yodelingly Yours Vol. 3 (Red Sleeve)

RCA Victor EPA-5097
The Legendary Jimmie Rodgers

(UK) RCA Victor RCX-1058 (EP)
The Legendary Jimmie Rodgers

(Australian) RCA 21002 (EP)

RCA Victor LPM-1232 Never No Mo' Blues

RCA Victor LPM-2112 My Rough And Rowdy Ways

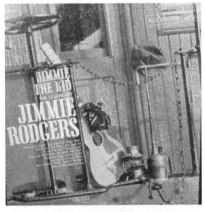

RCA Victor LPM-2213 Jimmie The Kid   RCA Victor LPM-2531 Country Music Hall Of Fame

RCA Victor LPM-2865 My Time Ain't Long   RCA Victor LPT-3073 Travellin' Blues By Jimmie Rodgers

RCA Victor LSP-3315 The Best Of The Legendary Jimmie Rodgers

 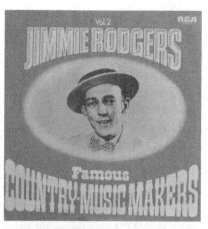

(UK) RCA DPS-2021 Famous Country Music Makers

(UK) RCA DPM-2047 Famous Country Music Makers Vol. 2

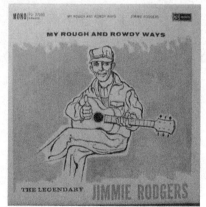

(UK) RCA RD-27203 My Rough And Rowdy Ways

Additional Recording Sessions

Own, vocal, guitar, dialogue

    Camden, New Jersey   October 30, 1929

    MVE-56970-1A, -2, -2A, -3, -3A, -4, -4A   The Singing Brakeman

- ❖ This recording was motion picture soundtrack for the film "The Singing Brakeman" – for Columbia Pictures
- ❖ This was a 16 inch Master
- ❖ Take 3 and 3A were renumbered MVE-58036 for foreign release
- ❖ It is not known which takes were used for the soundtrack

REGAL-ZONOPHONE Re-Mastering Session

Jimmie Rodgers not present

London, England   October 28, 1935

    WAR3690-1   Jimmie Rodgers Medley Part 1; Intro; My Old Pal; Dear Old Sunny South; Blue Yodel No. 1

    WAR3691-1   Jimmie Rodgers Medley Part 2; Intro; Daddy And Home; Away Out On The Mountain; Blue Yodel No. 4

Regal-Zonophone (Australia) G22792

Regal-Zonophone (Ireland) IZ414

Regal-Zonophone (UK) MR1918

Regal-Zonophone MR1918

VICTOR Overdub Session 1955

Jimmie Rodgers not present

As by Jimmie Rodgers & The Rainbow Ranch Boys

Nashville, Tennessee   March 18, 1955

    54864 (F2-WB-0281)   In The Jailhouse Now – No. 2

RCA Victor 20-6092

RCA Victor 47-6092 (45 RPM)

    54863 (F2-WB-0282)   Muleskinner Blues

RCA Victor 20-6205

VICTOR Overdub Session 1955 - *continued*

RCA Victor 47-6205 (45 RPM)

    58970 (F2-WB-0283)   Peach Picking Time In Georgia

RCA Victor 20-6092

RCA Victor 47-6092 (45 RPM)

    58961 (F2-WB-0284)   Mother, Queen Of My Heart

RCA Victor 20-6205

RCA Victor 47-6205 (45 RPM)

- ❖ "Peach Piking Time In Georgia" and "Mother, Queen Of My Heart" used the original accompanists on these recordings

As by Jimmie Rodgers & The Rainbow Ranch Boys

Nashville, Tennessee   July 22, 1955

    45099 (F2-WB-3952)   Never No Mo' Blues

RCA Victor 20-6408

RCA Victor 47-6408 (45 RPM)

    45095 (F2-WB-3954)   Daddy And Home

RCA Victor 20-6408

RCA Victor 47-6408 (45 RPM)

Unissued Tracks

You can find some of these unissued tracks on the ACM LP Series (Anthology Of Country Music) the tracks that can be found on either ACM-11 or ACM-12 are noted at the end of the track listing.

Note; You can now find many of these unissued tracks on CD.

1302-1	The Pullman Porters
Hollywood, California	July 17, 1930

Own, dialogue; Acc. I.N. Bronson, dialogue

❖ This is a comedy skit

40753 (F2-WB-3953)	Blue Yodel, #1 (T For Texas)
Nashville, Tennessee	July 22, 1955

❖ This was from the 1955 *Overdub Session* as by" Jimmie Rodgers And The Rainbow Ranch Boys"

41739-2	The Sailor's Plea
Camden, New Jersey	February 14, 1928

Own, vocal, yodel, guitar; Acc. The Three Southerners; Ellsworth T. Cozzens, steel guitar; Julian R. Ninde, guitar

ACM-11

40742 (F2-WB-3955)	Memphis Yodel
Nashville, Tennessee	July 22, 1955

❖ This was from the 1955 *Overdub Session* as by" Jimmie Rodgers And The Rainbow Ranch Boys"

45091-1	Mississippi Moon
Own, vocal, guitar;	
Camden, New Jersey	June 12, 1928

45091-3	Mississippi Moon
Own, vocal, guitar; Acc. Fred Koone, guitar	
Camden, New Jersey	June 12, 1928

45097-1   I'm Lonely And Blue

Own, vocal, guitar;

Dallas, Texas   February 5, 1932

ACM-12

48385-1   Any Old Time

Own, vocal, guitar; Acc. unknown, violin; unknown, clarinet; unknown, cornet; unknown, piano; unknown, tuba; unknown, traps;

New York City   February 21, 1929

ACM-12

49991   High Powered Mama

Own, vocal, guitar;

New York City   February 23, 1929

ACM-12

54849-3   My Blue Eyed Jane

Acc. Bob Sawyer's Jazz Band; unknown, cornet; unknown, clarinet; Bob Sawyer, piano; unknown, banjo; unknown, tuba;

Hollywood, California   June 30, 1930

54851-1   Moonlight And Skies

Acc. Lani McIntire's Hawaiian's; Sam Koki, steel guitar; Lani McIntire, guitar; unknown, ukulele; unknown, string bass;

Hollywood, California   June 30, 1930

ACM-11

54854-2   Take Me Back Again

Acc. Lani McIntire's Hawaiians; Sam Koki, steel guitar; Lani McIntire, guitar; unknown, ukulele; unknown, string bass;

Hollywood, California   July 2, 1930

ACM-11

54855-2   Those Gambler's Blues

Acc. Lani McIntire, guitar;

Hollywood, California   July 5, 1930

ACM-11

54856-1   I'm Lonesome Too

Own, vocal; Acc. Lani McIntire's Hawaiian's; Sam Koki, steel guitar; Lani McIntire, guitar; unknown, ukulele; unknown, string bass;

Hollywood, California   July 7, 1930

ACM-12

54860-1, -2   For The Sake Of Days Gone By

Own, vocal, yodel; Acc. Lani McIntire's Hawaiian's; Sam Koki, steel guitar; Lani McIntire, guitar; unknown, ukulele; unknown, string bass;

Hollywood, California   July 8, 1930

55333-1   Frankie And Johnny

Own, vocal, guitar;

Dallas, Texas   August 10, 1929

55344-3   Frankie And Johnny

Acc. unknown, cornet; unknown, saxophone; unknown, piano; unknown, banjo; unknown, string bass

Dallas, Texas   August 12, 1929

55345-2   Home Call

Own, guitar; Acc. Joe Kaipo, steel guitar; L.D. Dyke, saw

Dallas, Texas   August 12, 1929

55345-3   Home Call

Own, guitar; Acc. Joe Kaipo, steel guitar;

Dallas, Texas   August 12, 1929

56449-1 Whisper Your Mother's Name
Acc. Joe Kaipo, steel guitar; Billy Burkes, guitar; Weldon Burkes, ukulele
Dallas, Texas October 22, 1929

56449-4 Whisper Your Mother's Name
Acc. Joe Kaipo, steel guitar; Billy Burkes, guitar; Weldon Burkes, ukulele
Dallas, Texas October 22, 1929

56450-2 The Land Of My Boyhood Dreams
Own, guitar;
Dallas, Texas October 22, 1929

56450-3 The Land Of My Boyhood Dreams
Own, guitar;
Dallas, Texas October 22, 1929

56450-4 The Land Of My Boyhood Dreams
Own, guitar;
Dallas, Texas October 22, 1929

56453-1 Blue Yodel No. 6
Own, guitar;
Dallas, Texas October 22, 1929

56453-2 Blue Yodel No. 6
Own, guitar;
Dallas, Texas October 22, 1929

56455-2 My Rough And Rowdy Ways
Own, vocal, guitar; Acc. Joe Kaipo, steel guitar;
Dallas, Texas October 22, 1929

56455-3   My Rough And Rowdy Ways
Own, vocal, guitar; Acc. Joe Kaipo, steel guitar;
Dallas, Texas   October 22, 1929

56456-1   I've Ranged, I've Roamed, I've Travelled
Own, vocal, guitar;
Dallas, Texas   October 22, 1929

56456-2   I've Ranged, I've Roamed, I've Travelled
Own, vocal, guitar;
Dallas, Texas   October 22, 1929

56594-1   Mississippi River Blues
Acc. Billy Burkes, guitar
Atlanta, Georgia   November 25, 1929\

56607-2   Anniversary Blue Yodel (Blue Yodel No. 7)
Own, vocal, guitar; Acc. Billy Burkes, guitar
Atlanta, Georgia   November 26, 1929
ACM-12

56608-2   She Was Happy Till She Met You
Own, vocal; Acc. Billy Burkes, guitar
Atlanta, Georgia   November 26, 1929

56617-4   Blue Yodel, #11
Own, vocal, guitar; Billy Burkes, guitar
Atlanta, Georgia   November 27, 1929

56620-1   Why Did You Give Me Your Love?
Acc. Billy Burkes, guitar;
Atlanta, Georgia   November 28, 1929

58960-5 In The Hills Of Tennessee

Acc. Clayton McMichen, fiddle; Dave Kanui, steel guitar; Oddie McWinders, banjo; Hoyt "Slim" Bryant, guitar; George Howell, string bass;

Camden, New Jersey August 10, 1932

58962-1, -2 Prohibition Has Done Me Wrong

Acc. Clayton McMichen, fiddle; Oddie McWinders, banjo; Hoyt "Slim" Bryant, guitar;

Camden, New Jersey August 11, 1932

58964-1 Whippin' That Old T.B.

Acc. Clayton McMichen, fiddle; Oddie McWinders, banjo; Hoyt "Slim" Bryant, guitar;

Camden, New Jersey August 11, 1932

58968-3 No Hard Times

Own, guitar; Acc. Hoyt "Slim" Bryant, guitar;

Camden, New Jersey August 15, 1932

67133-2 T.B. Blues

Own, vocal, yodel, guitar; Acc. Charles Kama, steel guitar;

San Antonio, Texas January 31, 1931

67134-1 Travellin' Blues

Acc. Shelly Lee Alley, fiddle; Alvin Alley, fiddle; Charles Kama, steel guitar; M.T. Salazar, guitar; Mike Cordova, string bass;

San Antonio, Texas January 31, 1931

67134-3 Travellin' Blues

Acc. Shelly Lee Alley, fiddle; Alvin Alley, fiddle; Charles Kama, steel guitar; M.T. Salazar, guitar; Mike Cordova, string bass;

San Antonio, Texas January 31, 1931

67135-3 Jimmie The Kid

Acc. Charles Kama, steel guitar; M.T. Salazar, guitar; Mike Cordova, string bass;

San Antonio, Texas January 31, 1931

❖ *Acc. See VICTOR 23621 Note For Additional Information (Re-mastering Session only – Jimmie Rodgers not present)*

69032-1 Jimmie Rodgers' Puzzle Record

Camden, New Jersey November 11, 1931

❖ *Acc. See VICTOR 23621 Note For Additional Information (Re-mastering Session only – Jimmie Rodgers not present)*

69032-4 Rodgers' Puzzle Record

Camden, New Jersey November 11, 1931

69412-3 Why There's A Tear In My Eye

Vocal, yodel duet; Acc. Maybelle Carter, guitar;

Louisville, Kentucky June 10, 1931

69424-2 Let Me Be Your Side Track

Own, vocal, yodel; Clifford Gibson, guitar;

Louisville, Kentucky July 11, 1931

69424-4 Let Me Be Your Side Track

Own, vocal, yodel, guitar;

Louisville, Kentucky July 11, 1931

69427-1, -2 Jimmie Rodgers Visits The Carter Family

Own, vocal, yodel, speaking; Sara Carters, vocal, speaking, guitar; A.P. Carter, vocal, speaking; Maybelle Carter, vocal, speaking, mandolin, guitar;

Louisville, Kentucky June 11, 1931

69428 The Carter Family And Jimmie Rodgers In Texas

Own, vocal, yodel, speaking; Sara Carters, vocal, speaking, guitar; A.P. Carter, vocal, speaking; Maybelle Carter, vocal, speaking, mandolin, guitar;

Louisville, Kentucky   June 11, 1931

69432-3 When The Cactus Is In Bloom

Own, vocal, yodel; Acc. Cliff Carlisle, steel guitar; Wilbur Ball, guitar;

Louisville, Kentucky   June 13, 1931

69439-? Gambling Polka Dot Blues

Acc. Ruth Ann Moore, piano;

Louisville, Kentucky   June 15, 1931

❖ There are two different tracks issued under matrix 69439-? "Gambling Polka Dot Blues" on June 15, 1931

69443-1 Looking For A New Mama

Own, ukulele; Acc. Cliff Carlisle, steel guitar; Wilbur Ball, guitar;

Louisville, Kentucky   June 15, 1931

69448-? What's It?

Acc. Ruth Ann Moore, piano;

Louisville, Kentucky   June 16, 1931

69458-4 Southern Cannon-Ball

Own, guitar;

Louisville, Kentucky   June 16, 1931

ACM-11

69499-1 My Good Gal's Gone Blues

Acc. The Louisville Jug Band; Clifford Hayes, fiddle; George Allen, clarinet; Cal Smith, guitar; Freddie Smith, guitar; Earl McDonald, jug;

Louisville, Kentucky   June 16, 1931

70645-1   Roll Along Kentucky Moon

Own, vocal, yodel; Acc. Dick Bunyard, steel guitar; Red Young, mandolin; Bill Boyd, guitar' Fred Koone, string bass;

Dallas, Texas   February 2, 1932

70646-2   Hobo's Meditation

Acc. Dick Bunyard, steel guitar; Red Young, mandolin; Bill Boyd, guitar; Fred Koone, string bass

Dallas, Texas   February 3, 1932

70647-1   My Time Ain't Long

Own, guitar, vocal effects; Acc. Billy Burkes, steel guitar; Weldon Burkes, guitar; Fred Koone, string bass; Charlie Burkes, ukulele;

Dallas, Texas   February 4, 1932

70647-2   My Time Ain't Long

Own, guitar, vocal effects; Acc. Billy Burkes, steel guitar; Weldon Burkes, guitar; Fred Koone, string bass; Charlie Burkes, ukulele;

Dallas, Texas   February 4, 1932

76139-2   Dreaming With Tears In My Eyes

Own, guitar;

New York City   May 18, 1933

45 RPM Singles & EP's (Extended Play Records)

This section includes 45 RPM Singles and EP's released in the U.S., UK, and Australia

Note; This listing of 45 RPM Singles and EP's is not meant to be exhaustive, there are certainly additional 45 RPM Singles and EP's that have been released and that are not listed within this section. Most of the earlier issues that are not included are foreign releases. However some foreign and later U.S. releases have been excluded, some U.S. "Collector Series" and "Reissue Series" have also been excluded.

(U.S. Release)

RCA Victor 47-6092

54864-1	In The Jail-House Now – No. 2
58970-2A	Peach Pickin' Time Down In Georgia

RCA Victor 47-6205

54863-1	Blue Yodel No. 8 (Mule Skinner Blues)
58961-2A	Mother, Queen Of My Heart

RCA Victor 47-6408

45095-1	Daddy And Home
45099-1	Never No Mo' Blues

RCA Victor 599-9020

40753-2	Blue Yodel
40754-2	Away Out On The Mountain
45099-1	Never No Mo' Blues

RCA Victor EPA 6 "Jimmie Rodgers Immortal Performances"

Unknown Tracks Listing

RCA Victor EPA 10 "Jimmie Rodgers Vol. 1"

Unknown Tracks Listing

RCA Victor EPA 11 "Jimmie Rodgers Vol. 2"

Unknown Tracks Listing

RCA Victor EPA-21 "Yodelingy Yours" Volume 1

40753-2	Blue Yodel
40754-2	Away Out On The Mountain
41738-1	The Brakeman's Blues (Yodeling The Blues Away)
55333-2	Frankie And Johnny

RCA Victor EPA-22 "Yodelingy Yours" Volume 2

41743-2	Blue Yodel No. 3
45090-1	My Old Pal
48384-3	Desert Blues
49992-1	I'm Sorry We Met

RCA Victor EPA-23 "Yodelingy Yours" Volume 3

39768-3	Sleep, Baby, Sleep
41741-2	Blue Yodel – No. II (My Lovin' Gal Lucille)
47215-3	My Carolina Sunshine Girl
55308-1	Tuck Away My Lonesome Blue

RCA Victor EPA-409 "Jimmie Rodgers Memorial Album Vol. 4"

45095-1	Daddy And Home
45099-1	Never No Mo' Blues
47216-4	Blue Yodel No. 4 (California Blues)
47223-4	Waiting For A Train

RCA Victor EPA-410 "Jimmie Rodgers Memorial Album Vol. 5"

41736-1	Dear Old Sunny South By The Sea
54852-2	Pistol Packin' Papa
54861-3	Jimmie's Mean Mama Blues
56453-3	Blue Yodel No. 6

RCA Victor EPA-411 "Jimmie Rodgers Memorial Album Vol. 6"

    45096-1   My Little Lady

    45094-1   You And My Old Guitar

    Other Track Listings Unknown

RCA Victor EPA-793 "Never No Mo' Blues"

    45095-1   Daddy And Home

    45099-1   Never No Mo' Blues

    47216-4   Blue Yodel No. 4 (California Blues)

    47223-4   Waiting For A Train

RCA Victor EPA-5097 "The Legendary Jimmie Rodgers"

    40753-2   Blue Yodel (T For Texas)

    40754-2   Away Out On The Mountain

    41738-1   The Brakeman's Blues (Yodeling The Blues Away)

    47215-3   My Carolina Sunshine Girl

RCA EPB-1232 "Jimmie Rodgers Memorial Album" "Never No Mo' Blues" (2 EP Set)

547-0901

    45095-1   Daddy And Home

    45099-1   Never No Mo' Blues

    47216-4   Blue Yodel No. 4 (California Blues)

    47223-4   Waiting For A Train

547-0902

    73325-1   Prairie Lullaby

    56453-3   Blue Yodel No. 6

    54861-3   Jimmie's Mean Mama Blues

    76192-1   Old Pal Of My Heart

RCA Victor EPBT-3073 "Travellin' Blues By Jimmie Rodgers" (2 EP Set)
947-0225
55345-4	Home Call
67134-2	Travellin' Blues
54864-1	In The Jail-House Now No. 2
54863-1	Blue Yodel No. 8 (Mule Skinner Blues)

Titled as "Mule Skinner Blues" on the record

947-0226
58970-2A	Peach Pickin' Time Down In Georgia

Titles as "Peach Picking Time Down In Georgia" on the record

56607-1	Anniversary Blue Yodel (Blue Yodel No. 7)
73326-1	Miss The Mississippi And You
58961-2A	Mother, Queen Of My Heart

❖ This Double EP Set was also Released as an LP – LPT=3073

(Australian Release)

RCA EP-20176 (Australia Release)
41737-2	Treasures Untold
55309-2	Train Whistle Blues
56528-1	Hobo Bill's Last Ride

RCA EP-20219 (Australia Release)
40753-2	Blue Yodel
40754-2	Away Out On The Mountain
41738-1	The Brakeman's Blues (Yodeling The Blues Away)
47215-3	My Carolina Sunshine Girl

RCA EP-21002 (Australia Release)
45094-1	You And My Old Guitar
45095-1	Daddy And Home
45099-1	Never No Mo' Blues

(UK Release)

HMV 7EG-8163 (UK Release)

40753-2	Blue Yodel
40754-2	Away Out On The Mountain
41738-1	The Brakeman's Blues (Yodeling The Blues Away)
55333-2	Frankie And Johnny

RCA RCX-1058 (UK Release)

40753-2	Blue Yodel
40754-2	Away Out On The Mountain
41738-1	The Brakeman's Blues (Yodeling The Blues Away)
47215-3	My Carolina Sunshine Girl

LP'S

This section includes LP's released in the U.S., UK, Japan and Australia

Note; This listing of LP's is not meant to be exhaustive, there are certainly additional LP's that have been released and that are not listed within this section. Most of the earlier issues that are not included are foreign releases. However some foreign and later U.S. releases have been excluded.

(U.S. Release)

RCA Victor LPM-1232 "Jimmie Rodgers Memorial Album" "Never No Mo' Blues" (1955 Release)

41736-1	Dear Old Sunny South By The Sea
45094-1	You And My Old Guitar
45095-1	Daddy And Home
45096-1	My Little Lady
45099-1	Never No Mo' Blues
47216-4	Blue Yodel No. 4 (California Blues)
47223-4	Waiting For A Train
54852-2	Pistol Packin' Papa
54861-3	Jimmie's Mean Mama Blues
56453-3	Blue Yodel No. 6

RCA Victor LPM-1640 "Train Whistle Blues" (1957 Release)

40751-2	Ben Dewberry's Final Run
41737-2	Treasures Untold
45093-1	My Little Old Home Down In New Orleans
45098-2	Lullaby Yodel
48385-1	Any Old Time
49990-2	Blue Yodel No. 5
49991-2	High Powered Mama
55309-2	Train Whistle Blues
55332-2	Jimmie's Texas Blues
56528-1	Hobo Bill's Last Ride
69424-3	Let Me Be Your Side Track
69499-3	My Good Gal's Gone – Blues

RCA Victor LPM-2112 "My Rough And Rowdy Ways" The Legendary Jimmie Rodgers (1960 Release)

40753-2	Blue Yodel
40754-2	Away Out On The Mountain
41738-1	The Brakeman's Blues (Yodeling The Blues Away)
45091-5	Mississippi Moon
47215-3	My Carolina Sunshine Girl
54849-2	My Blue Eyed Jane
54857-1	The One Rose (That's Left In My Heart)
54863-1	Blue Yodel No. 8 (Mule Skinner Blues)
54864-1	In The Jail-House Now – No. 2
54867-2	Blue Yodel No. 9
56455-1	My Rough And Rowdy Ways
67134-2	Travellin' Blues
69458-1	Southern Cannon-Ball

RCA Victor LPM-2213 'Jimmie The Kid" (1961 Release)

39768-3	Sleep, Baby, Sleep
41741-2	Blue Yodel – No. II (My Lovin' Gal Lucille)
41743-2	Blue Yodel No. 3
45090-1	My Old Pal
48384-3	Desert Blues
49992-1	I'm Sorry We Met
55308-1	Tuck Away My Lonesome Blues
55333-2	Frankie And Johnny
55345-4	Home Call
56607-1	Anniversary Blue Yodel (Blue Yodel No. 7)
67135-1	Jimmie The Kid (Parts Of The Life Of Rodgers)
69443-3	Looking For A New Mama

RCA Victor LPM-2531 "Country Music Hall Of Fame" (1962 Release)

39767-4	The Soldier's Sweetheart
41739-1	The Sailor's Plea
54856-2	I'm Lonesome Too
54860-3	For The Sake Of Days Gone By
56454-3	Yodeling Cowboy
56594-3	Mississippi River Blues
56608-1	She Was Happy Till She Met You
67133-3	T.B. Blues
69432-2	When The Cactus Is In Bloom

RCA Victor LPM-2634 "The Short But Brilliant Life Of Jimmie Rodgers" (1963 Release)

41740-1	In The Jailhouse Now
47224-5	I'm Lonely And Blue
54850-3	Why Should I Be Lonely
54851-3	Moonlight And Skies
54854-3	Take Me Back Again
55307-2	Everybody Does It In Hawaii

LPM-2634 - *continued*

56595-4	Nobody Knows But Me
56617-1	Blue Yodel Number Eleven
56618-1	A Drunkard's Child

RCA Victor LPM- 2865 "My Time Ain't Long"

40752	My Mother Was A Lady
54855-1	Those Gambler's Blues
54862-3	The Mystery Of Number Five
56450-1	The Land Of My Boyhood Dreams
56456-3	I've Ranged, I've Roamed, I've Travelled
56619-1	That's Why I'm Blue
56620-3	Why Did You Give Me Your Love?
69412-3 (Previously Unissued)	Why There's A Tear In My Eye
69413-2 (with Sara Carter)	The Wonderful City
69427-4	Jimmie Rodgers Visits The Carter Family
69428-4 (with The Carter Family)	The Carter Family And Jimmie Rodgers In Texas
69439-2	Gambling Polka Dot Blues
69448-1	What's It?

RCA Victor LPT-3037

40753-2	Blue Yodel
40754-2	Away Out On The Mountain
41738-1	The Brakeman's Blues (Yodeling The Blues Away)
41743-2	Blue Yodel No. 3
45090-1	My Old Pal
48384-3	Desert Blues
49992-1	I'm Sorry We Met
55333-2	Frankie And Johnny

RCA Victor LPT-3038

39768-3	Sleep, Baby, Sleep
41741-2	Blue Yodel – No. II (My Lovin' Gal Lucille)
45095-1	Daddy And Home
45099-1	Never No Mo' Blues
47215-3	My Carolina Sunshine Girl
47216-4	Blue Yodel No. 4 (California Blues)
47223-4	Waiting For A Train
55308-1	Tuck Away My Lonesome Blues

RCA Victor LPT-3039

41736-1	Dear Old Sunny South By The Sea
45094-1	You And My Old Guitar
45096-1	My Little Lady
54852-2	Pistol Packin' Papa
54861-3	Jimmie's Mean Mama Blues
56453-3	Blue Yodel No. 6

RCA Victor LPT-3073 "Travellin' Blues By Jimmie Rodgers"

55345-4	Home Call
67134-2	Travellin' Blues
54867-2	Blue Yodel No. 9
54863-1	Mule Skinner Blues (Blue Yodel No. 8)
58970-2A	Peach Picking Time Down In Georgia
56607-1	Anniversary Blue Yodel (Blue Yodel No. 7)
73326-1	Miss The Mississippi And You
58961-2A	Mother, Queen Of My Heart

❖ This LP was also released as a double EP Set EPBT-3073

RCA Victor LSP-3315 "The Best Of The Legendary Jimmie Rodgers" (1965 Release)

40753-2	Blue Yodel
40754-2	Away Out On The Mountain

LSP-3315 - *continued*

45095-1	Daddy And Home
47223-4	Waiting For A Train
48385-1	Any Old Time
54850-3	Why Should I Be Lonely
54851-3	Moonlight And Skies
54862-3	The Mystery Of Number Five
54863-1	Blue Yodel No. 8 (Mule Skinner Blues)
56619-1	That's Why I'm Blue
56620-3	Why Did You Give Me Your Love?

RCA Victor VPS-6091(e) "This Is Jimmie Rodgers" (2 LP Set)
(1973 Release)

40753-2	Blue Yodel
40754-2	Away Out On The Mountain
41736-1	Dear Old Sunny South By The Sea
41737-2	Treasures Untold
41738-1	The Brakeman's Blues (Yodeling The Blues Away)
41740-1	In The Jailhouse Now
45090-1	My Old Pal
45095-1	Daddy And Home
45099-1	Never No Mo' Blues
47215-3	My Carolina Sunshine Girl
47216-4	Blue Yodel No. 4 (California Blues)
47223-4	Waiting For A Train
48385-1	Any Old Time
54852-2	Pistol Packin' Papa
54863-1	Blue Yodel No. 8 (Mule Skinner Blues)
54864-1	In The Jail-House Now – No. 2
55333-2	Frankie And Johnny
56455-1	My Rough And Rowdy Ways

RCA Victor DPL 2-0075 "The Legendary Jimmie Rodgers Vol. 1" (1974 Release)

❖ This was a "Special Products" issue for Country Music Magazine

39767-4	The Soldier's Sweetheart
40753-2	Blue Yodel
40754-2	Away Out On The Mountain
41736-1	Dear Old Sunny South By The Sea
41740-1	In The Jailhouse Now
45093-1	My Little Old Home Down In New Orleans
47215-3	My Carolina Sunshine Girl
47216-4	Blue Yodel No. 4 (California Blues)
48385-1	Any Old Time
54849-2	My Blue Eyed Jane
54851-3	Moonlight And Skies
55333-2	Frankie And Johnny
56455-1	My Rough And Rowdy Ways
56456-3	I've Ranged, I've Roamed, I've Travelled
67135-1	Jimmie The Kid (Parts Of The Life Of Rodgers)
69428-4 (with The Carter Family)	The Carter Family And Jimmie Rodgers In Texas

RCA Camden ACL-7029

40753-2	Blue Yodel
40754-2	Away Out On The Mountain
41738-1	The Brakeman's Blues (Yodeling The Blues Away)
41743-2	Blue Yodel No. 3
45090-1	My Old Pal
48384-3	Desert Blues
49992-1	I'm Sorry We Met
55333-2	Frankie And Johnny

ACM – 11 (Anthology Of Country Music) "The Unissued Jimmie Rodgers Vol. 1"

41739-2 (*Previously Unissued*)	The Sailor's Plea
54851-1(*Previously Unissued*)	Moonlight And Skies
54854-2(*Previously Unissued*)	Take Me Back Again
54855-2(*Previously Unissued*)	Those Gambler's Blues

56449-1 (this take was originally issued on Victor 22319) Whisper Your Mother's Name

56620-1 (this take was originally issued on Bluebird B-5862) Why Did You Give Me Your Love?

69427-1, -2 (Unknown which take was used) Jimmie Rodgers Visits The Carter Family

69428-4 (this take was originally issued on Bluebird B-6762) The Carter Family And Jimmie Rodgers In Texas

69439-? (Unknown which take was used) Gambling Polka Dot Blues

69448-? (Unknown which take was used) What's It?

69499-3 (this take was originally issued on Bluebird B-5942) My Good Gal's Gone Blues

69458-4(*Previously Unissued*)	Southern Cannon-Ball

ACM – 12 (Anthology Of Country Music) "The Unheard Jimmie Rodgers Vol. 2"

45097-1(*Previously Unissued*)	I'm Lonely And Blue
48385-1(*Previously Unissued*)	Any Old Time
49991 (*Previously Unissued*)	High Powered Mama
54856-1(*Previously Unissued*)	I'm Lonesome Too

54864-1 (this take was originally issued on Victor 22523)

In The Jail-House Now, No. 2

56450-1 (this take was originally issued on Victor 23811)

The Land Of My Boyhood Dreams

56453-3 (this take was originally issued on Victor 22271)

Blue Yodel No. 6

56456-3 (this take was originally issued on Bluebird B-5892)

ACM – 12 -*continued*

    I've Ranged, I've Roamed And I've Travelled

    56594-3 (this take was originally issued on Victor 23535)

    Mississippi River Blues

    56607-2 (Previously Unissued)   Anniversary Blue Yodel (Blue Yodel No. 7)

    69439-? (Unknown which take was used) Gambling Polka Dot Blues

AHL1-3315 Reissue of "RCA Victor LSP-3315 "The Best Of The Legendary Jimmie Rodgers" (197? Release)

ANL1-1209 Reissue of "RCA Victor LPM-2112 "My Rough And Rowdy Ways" (1976 Release)

                      (UK Release)

RCA DPS – 2021 (UK Release) Famous Country Music-Makers (2 LP)

39768-3	Sleep, Baby, Sleep
40751-2	Ben Dewberry's Final Run
41737-2	Treasures Untold
41741-2	Blue Yodel – No. II (My Lovin' Gal Lucille)
41743-2	Blue Yodel No. 3
45090-1	My Old Pal
45093-1	My Little Old Home Down In New Orleans
45098-2	Lullaby Yodel
48384-3	Desert Blues
48385-1	Any Old Time
49990-2	Blue Yodel No. 5
49991-2	High Powered Mama
49992-1	I'm Sorry We Met
55308-1	Tuck Away My Lonesome Blues
55309-2	Train Whistle Blues
55332-2	Jimmie's Texas Blues

DPS-2021 - *continued*

55333-2	Frankie And Johnny
55345-4	Home Call
56528-1	Hobo Bill's Last Ride
56607-1	Anniversary Blue Yodel (Blue Yodel No. 7)
67135-1	Jimmie The Kid (Parts Of The Life Of Rodgers)
69424-3	Let Me Be Your Side Track
69443-3	Looking For A New Mama
69499-1	My Good Gal's Gone – Blues

RCA DPM-2047 (UK Release) Famous Country Music-Makers Vol. 2

39767-4	The Soldier's Sweetheart
40753-2	Blue Yodel
40754-2	Away Out On The Mountain
41736-1	Dear Old Sunny South By The Sea
45094-1	You And My Old Guitar
47215-3	My Carolina Sunshine Girl
54852-2	Pistol Packin' Papa
54860-3	For The Sake Of Days Gone By
54862-3	The Mystery Of Number Five
56449-3	Whisper Your Mother's Name
56450-1	The Land Of My Boyhood Dreams
56453-3	Blue Yodel No. 6
56594-3	Mississippi River Blues
56617-1	Blue Yodel Number Eleven
56618-1	A Drunkard's Child
56620-3	Why Did You Give Me Your Love?
67134-2	Travellin' Blues
69412-3 (Previously Unissued)	Why There's A Tear In My Eye
69413-2 (with Sara Carter)	The Wonderful City
69432-2	When The Cactus Is In Bloom
69458-1	Southern Cannon-Ball

RCA RD 7505 (UK Release)

39767-4	The Soldier's Sweetheart
41739-1	The Sailor's Plea
54856-2	I'm Lonesome Too
54860-3	For The Sake Of Days Gone By
56454-3	Yodeling Cowboy
56594-3	Mississippi River Blues
56608-1	She Was Happy Till She Met You
67133-3	T.B. Blues
69432-2	When The Cactus Is In Bloom

RCA RD 7562 (UK Release) "The Short But Brilliant Life Of Jimmie Rodgers"

41740-1	In The Jailhouse Now
47224-5	I'm Lonely And Blue
54850-3	Why Should I Be Lonely
54851-3	Moonlight And Skies
54854-3	Take Me Back Again
55307-2	Everybody Does It In Hawaii
56595-4	Nobody Knows But Me
56617-1	Blue Yodel Number Eleven
56618-1	A Drunkard's Child

RCA RD 7644 (UK Release)

40752	My Mother Was A Lady
54855-1	Those Gambler's Blues
54862-3	The Mystery Of Number Five
56450-1	The Land Of My Boyhood Dreams
56456-3	I've Ranged, I've Roamed, I've Travelled
56619-1	That's Why I'm Blue
56620-3	Why Did You Give Me Your Love?
69412-3 (Previously Unissued)	Why There's A Tear In My Eye
69413-2 (with Sara Carter)	The Wonderful City

RD-7644 - *continued*

69427-4	Jimmie Rodgers Visits The Carter Family
69428-4 (with The Carter Family) Jimmie Rodgers In Texas	The Carter Family And
69439-2	Gambling Polka Dot Blues
69448-1	What's It?

RCA RD-27110 (UK Release)

40751-2	Ben Dewberry's Final Run
41737-2	Treasures Untold
45093-1	My Little Old Home Down In New Orleans
45098-2	Lullaby Yodel
48385-1	Any Old Time
49990-2	Blue Yodel No. 5
49991-2	High Powered Mama
55309-2	Train Whistle Blues
55332-2	Jimmie's Texas Blues
56528-1	Hobo Bill's Last Ride
69424-3	Let Me Be Your Side Track
69499-3	My Good Gal's Gone – Blues

RCA RD-27138 (UK Release)

41736-1	Dear Old Sunny South By The Sea
45094-1	You And My Old Guitar
45095-1	Daddy And Home
45096-1	My Little Lady
45099-1	Never No Mo' Blues
47216-4	Blue Yodel No. 4 (California Blues)
47223-4	Waiting For A Train
54852-2	Pistol Packin' Papa
54861-3	Jimmie's Mean Mama Blues
56453-3	Blue Yodel No. 6

RCA RD-27203 (UK Release) My Rough And Rowdy Ways The Legendary Jimmie Rodgers

54849-2	My Blue Eyed Jane
54857-1	The One Rose (That's Left In My Heart)
54863-1	Blue Yodel No. 8 (Mule Skinner Blues)
54864-1	In The Jail-House Now – No. 2
54867-2	Blue Yodel No. 9
56455-1	My Rough And Rowdy Ways
67134-2	Travellin' Blues
69458-1	Southern Cannon-Ball

RCA RD-27241 (UK Release)

39768-3	Sleep, Baby, Sleep
41741-2	Blue Yodel – No. II (My Lovin' Gal Lucille)
41743-2	Blue Yodel No. 3
45090-1	My Old Pal
48384-3	Desert Blues
49992-1	I'm Sorry We Met
55308-1	Tuck Away My Lonesome Blues
55345-4	Home Call
67135-1	Jimmie The Kid (Parts Of The Life Of Rodgers)
69443-3	Looking For A New Mama

(Japan Release)

RCA RA-5176 (Japan Release)

39768-3	Sleep, Baby, Sleep
40753-2	Blue Yodel
41736-1	Dear Old Sunny South By The Sea
41737-2	Treasures Untold
45098-2	Lullaby Yodel
45099-1	Never No Mo' Blues
48385-1	Any Old Time

RA-5176 - *continued*

54857-1	The One Rose (That's Left In My Heart)
54863-1	Blue Yodel No. 8 (Mule Skinner Blues)
54867-2	Blue Yodel No. 9
56528-1	Hobo Bill's Last Ride

RCA RA-5459 (Japan Release)

39767-4	The Soldier's Sweetheart
39768-3	Sleep, Baby, Sleep
40751-2	Ben Dewberry's Final Run
40752	My Mother Was A Lady
40753-2	Blue Yodel
40754-2	Away Out On The Mountain
41736-1	Dear Old Sunny South By The Sea
41737-2	Treasures Untold
41738-1	The Brakeman's Blues (Yodeling The Blues Away)
41739-1	The Sailor's Plea
41740-1	In The Jailhouse Now
41741-2	Blue Yodel – No. II (My Lovin' Gal Lucille)
41743-2	Blue Yodel No. 3

RCA RA-5460 (Japan Release)

45090-1	My Old Pal
45093-1	My Little Old Home Down In New Orleans
45094-1	You And My Old Guitar
45095-1	Daddy And Home
45096-1	My Little Lady
45098-2	Lullaby Yodel
45099-1	Never No Mo' Blues
47215-3	My Carolina Sunshine Girl
47216-4	Blue Yodel No. 4 (California Blues)
47223-4	Waiting For A Train
47224-5	I'm Lonely And Blue

RA-5460 - *continued*

48384-3	Desert Blues
48385-1	Any Old Time
49990-2	Blue Yodel No. 5

RCA RA-5462 (Japan Release)

54849-2	My Blue Eyed Jane
54850-3	Why Should I Be Lonely
54851-3	Moonlight And Skies
54852-2	Pistol Packin' Papa
54854-2	Take Me Back Again
56594-3	Mississippi River Blues
56595-4	Nobody Knows But Me
56607-1	Anniversary Blue Yodel (Blue Yodel No. 7)
56608-1	She Was Happy Till She Met You
56617-1	Blue Yodel Number Eleven
56618-1	A Drunkard's Child
56620-3	Why Did You Give Me Your Love?

RCA RA-5463 (Japan Release)

54855-1	Those Gambler's Blues
54856-2	I'm Lonesome Too
54857-1	The One Rose (That's Left In My Heart)
54860-3	For The Sake Of Days Gone By
54861-3	Jimmie's Mean Mama Blues
54862-3	The Mystery Of Number Five
54863-1	Blue Yodel No. 8 (Mule Skinner Blues)
54864-1	In The Jail-House Now – No. 2
54867-2	Blue Yodel No. 9
67133-3	T.B. Blues
67134-2	Travellin' Blues
67135-1	Jimmie The Kid (Parts Of The Life Of Rodgers)
69412-3 (Previously Unissued)	Why There's A Tear In My Eye

RCA RA-5501 (Japan Release)

40754-2	Away Out On The Mountain
45096-1	My Little Lady
47223-4	Waiting For A Train
54864-1	In The Jail-House Now – No. 2
55333-2	Frankie And Johnny
67135-1	Jimmie The Kid (Parts Of The Life Of Rodgers)
69412-3 (Previously Unissued)	Why There's A Tear In My Eye
69413-2 (with Sara Carter)	The Wonderful City
69427-4	Jimmie Rodgers Visits The Carter Family
69428-4 (with The Carter Family)	The Carter Family And Jimmie Rodgers In Texas
69458-1	Southern Cannon-Ball

RCA RA-5510 (Japan Release)

39768-3	Sleep, Baby, Sleep
40753-2	Blue Yodel
41736-1	Dear Old Sunny South By The Sea
41737-2	Treasures Untold
45098-2	Lullaby Yodel
45099-1	Never No Mo' Blues
48385-1	Any Old Time
54851-3	Moonlight And Skies
54857-1	The One Rose (That's Left In My Heart)
54863-1	Blue Yodel No. 8 (Mule Skinner Blues)
54867-2	Blue Yodel No. 9
56528-1	Hobo Bill's Last Ride

RCA RA-9037 (Japan Release)

39768-3	Sleep, Baby, Sleep
40753-2	Blue Yodel
41736-1	Dear Old Sunny South By The Sea
45098-2	Lullaby Yodel

RA-9037 - *continued*

47215-3	My Carolina Sunshine Girl
47216-4	Blue Yodel No. 4 (California Blues)
47223-4	Waiting For A Train
48385-1	Any Old Time
55309-2	Train Whistle Blues
55332-2	Jimmie's Texas Blues
55333-2	Frankie And Johnny
56528-1	Hobo Bill's Last Ride

RCA RA-9038 (Japan Release)

54850-3	Why Should I Be Lonely
54857-1	The One Rose (That's Left In My Heart)
54863-1	Blue Yodel No. 8 (Mule Skinner Blues)
56594-3	Mississippi River Blues
69432-2	When The Cactus Is In Bloom

(Australia Release)

RCA L-10883 (Australia Release)

40753-2	Blue Yodel
40754-2	Away Out On The Mountain
41738-1	The Brakeman's Blues (Yodeling The Blues Away)
47215-3	My Carolina Sunshine Girl
54849-2	My Blue Eyed Jane
54857-1	The One Rose (That's Left In My Heart)
54863-1	Blue Yodel No. 8 (Mule Skinner Blues)
54864-1	In The Jail-House Now – No. 2
54867-2	Blue Yodel No. 9
56455-1	My Rough And Rowdy Ways
67134-2	Travellin' Blues
69458-1	Southern Cannon-Ball

Jimmie Rodgers Song Writing Credits

This listing shows the song title first, the first known recorded date by Jimmie Rodgers and the first record label and catalogue number issued when released

A Drunkard's Child *(Co-written with Andrew Jenkins)*
    Recorded 11/28/1929
    Victor 22319

Anniversary Blue Yodel *(Co-written with Elsie McWilliams)*
    Recorded 11/26/1929
    Victor 22488

Any Old Time
    Recorded 2/21/1929
    Victor 22488

Blue Yodel
    Recorded 11/30/1927
    Victor 21142

Blue Yodel No. II
    Recorded 2/15/1928
    Victor 21291

Blue Yodel No. 3
    Recorded 2/15/1928
    Victor 21531

Blue Yodel No. 4
    Recorded 10/20/1928
    Victor V-40014

Blue Yodel No. 5
>   Recorded 2/23/1929
>   Victor 22072

Blue Yodel No. 6
>   Recorded 10/22/1929
>   Victor 22271

Blue Yodel No. 11 (Number Eleven)
>   Recorded 11/27/1929
>   Victor 23796

Brakeman's Blues, The
>   Recorded 2/14/1928
>   Victor 21291

Carter Family And Jimmie Rodgers In Texas, The
>   Recorded 6/11/1931
>   Bluebird B-6762

Daddy And Home *(Co-written with Elsie McWilliams)*
>   Recorded 6/12/1928
>   Victor 21757

Desert Blues
>   Recorded 2/21/1929
>   Victor V-40096

Everybody Does It In Hawaii *(Co-written with Elsie McWilliams)*
>   Recorded 8/8/1929
>   Victor 22143

For The Sake Of Days Gone By *(Co-written with Jack White)*
    Recorded 7/8/1930
    Victor 23651

Gambling Polka Dot Blues *(Co-written with Raymond E. Hall)*
    Recorded 6/15/1931
    Victor 23636

High Powered Mama
    Recorded 2/23/1929
    Victor 22523

Home Call *(Co-written with Elsie McWilliams)*
    Recorded 8/12/1929
    Victor 23681

I'm Lonely And Blue *(Co-written with Elsie McWilliams)*
    Recorded 6/12/1928
    Victor V-40054

I'm Lonesome Too
    Recorded 7/71930
    Victor 23564

I'm Sorry We Met
    Recorded 2/23/1929
    Victor 22072

In The Jailhouse Now
    Recorded 2/15/1928
    Victor 21245

I've Ranged, I've Roamed And I've Travelled *(Co-written with Elsie McWilliams)*
>Recorded 10/22/1929
>Bluebird B-5892

Jimmie The Kid *(Co-written with Jack Neville)*
>Recorded 1/31/1931
>Victor 23549

Jimmie's Texas Blues
>Recorded 8/10/1929
>Victor 22379

Land Of My Boyhood Dreams, The
>Recorded 10/22/1929
>Victor 23811

Lullaby Yodel *(Co-written with Elsie McWilliams)*
>Recorded 6/12/1928
>Victor 21636

Memphis Yodel
>Recorded 2/15/1928
>Victor 21636

Mississippi Moon *(Co-written with Elsie McWilliams)*
>Recorded 6/12/1928
>Victor 23696

Mississippi River Blues
>Recorded 11/25/1929
>Victor 23535

Moonlight And Skies *(Co-written with Raymond E. Hall)*
- Recorded 6/30/1930
- Victor 23574

My Blue Eyed Jane *(Co-written with Lulu Belle White)*
- Recorded 6/30/1930
- Victor 23549

My Carolina Sunshine Girl
- Recorded 10/20/1928
- Victor V-40096

My Little Lady *(Co-written with Elsie McWilliams)*
- Recorded 6/12/1928
- Victor V-40072

My Little Old Home Down In New Orleans
- Recorded 6/12/1928
- Victor 21574

My Old Pal *(Co-written with Elsie McWilliams)*
- Recorded 6/12/1928
- Victor 21757

My Rough And Rowdy Ways *(Co-written with Elsie McWilliams)*
- Recorded 10/22/1929
- Victor 22220

Never No Mo' Blues *(Co-written with Elsie McWilliams)*
- Recorded 6/12/1928
- Victor 21531

Nobody Knows But Me *(Co-written with Elsie McWilliams)*
>   Recorded 11/25/1929
>   Victor 23518

Pistol Packin' Papa *(Co-written with Waldo Lafayette O'Neal)*
>   Recorded 7/1/1930
>   Victor 22554

Sailor's Plea, The *(Co-written with Elsie McWilliams)*
>   Recorded 1928
>   Victor V-40054

She Was Happy Till She Met You *(Co-written with Elsie McWilliams)*
>   Recorded 11/26/1929
>   Victor 23681

Soldiers Sweetheart, The
>   Recorded 8/4/1927
>   Victor 20864

Southern Cannon-Ball *(Co-written with Raymond E. Hall)*
>   Recorded 6/17/1931
>   Victor 23811

Take Me Back Again *(Co-written with Raymond E. Hall)*
>   Recorded 7/2/1930
>   Bluebird B-7600

That's Why I'm Blue *(Co-written with Elsie McWilliams)*
>   Recorded 11/28/1929
>   Victor 22421

Train Whistle Blues
>	Recorded 8/8/1929
>	Victor 22379

Travellin' Blues *(Co-written with Shelly Lee Alley)*
>	Recorded 1/31/1931
>	Victor 23564

Treasures Untold *(Ellswoth T. Cozzens – composer)*
>	Recorded 2/14/1928
>	Victor 21433

Tuck Away My Lonesome Blues *(Co-written with Elsie McWilliams & Joe Kaipo)*
>	Recorded 8/8/1929
>	Victor 22220

Waiting For A Train
>	Recorded 10/22/1928
>	Victor V-40014

What's It? *(Co-written with Jack Neville)*
>	Recorded 5/15/1931
>	Victor 23609

Whisper Your Mother's Name
>	Recorded 10/22/1929
>	Victor 22319

Why Did You Give Me Your Love?
>	Recorded 11/28/1929
>	Bluebird B-5892

Why Should I Be Lonely? *(Co-written with Estelle Lovell)*
    Recorded 6/30/1930
    Victor 23609

Wonderful City, The *(Co-written with Elsie McWilliams)*
    Recorded 6/10/1931
    Bluebird B-6810

Yodeling Cowboy *(Co-written with Elsie McWilliams)*
    Recorded 10/22/1929
    Victor 22271

You And My Old Guitar *(Co-written with Elsie McWilliams))*
    Recorded 6/12/1928
    Victor V-40072

Bibliography

In Tune: Charley Patton And Jimmie Rodgers And The Roots Of American Music; by Ben Wynne – Louisiana State University Press 2014

Jimmie Rodgers: The Life And Times Of America's Blue Yodeler; By Nolan Porterfield – Published by University Press of Mississippi 2007

Country Music Originals: The Legends And The Lost; By Tony Russell – Oxford University Press 2008

Country Music Records: A Discography 1921-1942: by Tony Russell & Bob Pinson - Oxford University Press, USA 2008

Country Music Records; By Jerry Osborne – House Of Collectibles 1996

The Encyclopedia Of Country Music; Michael McCall, Paul Kingsbury, John Rumble – Oxford University Press 2012

The Almost Complete 78 RPM Dating Guide; By Steven C. Barr – Published By Yesterday Once Again 1992

American Record Labels And Companies An Encyclopedia (1891 – 1943); By Allan Sutton & Kurt Nauck – Mainspring Press 2000

American Premium Record Guide 1900-1965 6th Edition: by Les Docks – Krause Publications, Books Americana, Iola, WI 2001

Country & Western Record Price Guide; By Tim Neely – Krause Publications 2001

The Folk Music Sourcebook; By Larry Sanders & Dick Weissman – Published by AlfredA. Knopf 1976

B.J.'s Country & Rock N Roll Collectors Guide; By Barry K. John – B.J. Publications, Phoenix, Arizona 2000

Performer Index

An "*" next to the page number informs you that there is more than one mention of that performers name on that same page.

Allen, George, 49, 76, 110

Alley, Alvin, 24, 75, 108*

Alley, Shelly Lee, 24, 75, 108*

Armstrong, Lillian (Hardin), 25, 63

Armstrong, Louis, 25, 63

Ball, Wilbur, 25, 27, 41, 44, 55, 57, 60, 65, 79, 83, 110

Boyd, Bill, 28, 30, 43, 61, 66, 82, 111*

Bryan, Dean, 37*, 38, 39, 44, 46, 57, 58, 66, 70, 72, 78*, 83

Bryant, Hoyt "Slim", 31*, 32*, 33*, 34, 40, 41*, 42*, 48, 52, 54*, 55*, 56*, 59*, 60*, 61*, 62, 74, 77, 79, 80*, 81*, 108*

Bunyard, Dick, 28, 30, 43, 61, 66, 82, 111*

Burkes, Billy, 17*, 18*, 19*, 20*, 22, 23, 28, 29, 34, 41, 43, 44, 46, 47, 49, 50, 55, 56*, 62, 63*, 64, 65, 67*, 68, 72, 73, 74, 76*, 80, 82, 83, 106*, 107*, 111*

Burkes, Charlie, 65, 111*

Burkes, Weldon, 17*, 18*, 19, 28, 29, 41, 43, 44, 47, 55, 56*, 62, 65, 67*, 68, 76, 80, 82, 83, 106*, 111*

Cali, John, 35, 36*, 50

Carlisle, Cliff, 25, 27, 41, 44, 55, 57, 60, 65, 79, 83, 110

Carter, A.P., 25, 52, 72, 77, 109, 110

Carter, Maybelle, 25, 51, 52*, 72, 77*, 109*, 110

Carter, Sara, 25, 51, 52*, 72, 77*, 109, 110

Carter Family, The, 25, 52

Colicchio, Tony, 35, 36*, 50, 71*

Cordova, Mike, 23, 24, 75*, 108*, 109

Cozzens, Ellsworth T., 12, 13*, 15*, 38, 45, 48, 51*, 53, 57, 64*, 65, 70, 72, 73, 76, 78, 84, 103

Dyke, L. D., 105

Gibson, Clifford, 109

Hardin, Lillian - See Armstrong, Lillian (Hardin)

Hayes, Clifford, 49, 76, 110

Howell, George, 108

Hutchison, C.L., 37*, 38, 39, 44, 46, 57, 58, 66, 70, 72, 78*, 83

Kaipo, Joe, 17*, 18*, 19*, 29, 41, 47, 55, 64, 65, 68, 76, 80, 105*, 106*, 107

Kama, Charles, 23*, 51, 59, 75*, 108*, 109

Kanui, Dave, 108

Koki, Sam, 24*, 26, 28, 40, 42, 48*, 52, 53, 54*, 61, 65, 67*, 70, 79, 81, 104*, 105*

Koone, Fred, 28, 29, 30*, 42, 43*, 44, 56*, 60, 61, 65, 66, 67*, 81, 82*, 83, 103, 111*

Louisville Jug Band, The, 49, 76, 110

MacGimsey, Bob, 17, 19, 47 68, 76

MacMillan, George, 37*, 38, 39, 44, 46, 57, 58, 66, 70, 72, 78*, 83

142

McDonald, Earl, 49, 76, 110

McIntire, Lani, 21, 24*, 26, 28, 40, 42, 48*, 52, 53, 54*, 61, 63, 65, 67*, 70, 79, 81, 104*, 105*

McIntire's, Lani Hawaiians, 24*, 26, 28, 40, 42, 48*, 52, 53, 54*, 61, 65, 67*, 70, 79, 81, 104*, 105*

McMichen, Clayton, 31*, 32*, 33*, 40, 41*, 42*, 52, 54*, 55*, 56*, 59*, 60, 61*, 77, 79, 80*, 81*, 108*

McWinders, Oddie, 31*, 32, 33*, 40, 41*, 42*, 52, 54*, 55*, 56*, 59*, 60*, 61*, 77, 79, 80*, 81*, 108*

Moore, Ruth Ann, 26, 27, 43, 62, 82, 110

Ninde, Julian R., 13, 15, 38, 48, 51*, 53, 65, 76, 103

Rainbow Ranch Boys, The, 101, 102

Rikard, James, 37*, 39, 44, 46, 57, 70, 72, 78, 83

Salazar, M.T., 23, 24, 75*, 108*, 109

Sawyer, Bob, 22*, 23, 46, 51, 68, 73*, 79, 104

Sawyer's, Bob Jazz band, 22*, 23, 46, 51, 68, 73*, 79, 104

Smith, Cal, 49, 76, 110

Smith, Freddie, 49, 76, 110

Three Southerners, The, 13*, 15, 38, 48, 51*, 53, 64, 65, 76, 103

Westbrook, John, 37*, 38, 39, 44, 46, 57, 58, 66, 70, 72, 78*, 83

Young, Red, 28, 30, 43, 61, 66, 82, 111*

Song Index

An "" next to the page number informs you that there is more than one mention of that performers name on that same page.*

A Drunkard's Child, 18, 19, 67, 119, 125, 126, 130, 133

Anniversary Blue Yodel (Blue Yodel No. 7), 20, 63, 107, 115, 118, 120, 124, 125, 130, 133

Any Old Time, 20, 47, 75, 104, 117, 121*, 122, 123, 124, 127, 128, 130, 131, 132, 133

Away Out On The Mountain, 12, 44, 58, 83, 101, 112, 113, 114, 115, 116*, 117, 119, 120, 121, 122*, 125, 129, 131, 132

Ben Dewberry's Final Run, 12, 46, 117, 124, 127, 129

Blue Yodel #1 (T For Texas), 103, 114

Blue Yodel (No. 1), 12, 58, 83, 101, 112, 113, 115, 116*, 117, 119, 120, 121, 122*, 125, 128*, 129, 131*, 132, 133

Blue Yodel – No. II (My Lovin' Gal Lucille), 13, 64, 78, 113, 118, 120, 124, 128, 129, 133

Blue Yodel No. 3, 14, 64, 113, 118, 119, 122, 124, 128, 129, 133

Blue Yodel No. 4 (California Blues), 37, 72, 78, 101, 113, 114*, 116, 120, 121, 122, 127, 129, 132, 133

Blue Yodel No. 5, 16, 64, 117, 124, 127, 130, 134

Blue Yodel No. 6, 18, 63, 106*, 113, 114, 116, 120, 123, 125, 127, 134

Blue Yodel No. 7 (see *Anniversary Blue Yodel*)

Blue Yodel No. 8 (Mule Skinner Blues), 22, 51, 73, 79, 112, 115, 117, 120, 121*, 128, 129, 130, 131, 132

Blue Yodel No. 9, 25, 63, 117, 120, 128, 129, 130, 131, 132

Blue Yodel No. 10 (Ground Hog Rootin' In My Back Yard), 30, 62, 73, 74

Blue Yodel #11 (see also *Blue Yodel No. 11*), 107

Blue Yodel No. 11 (see *Blue Yodel Number Eleven* & *Blue Yodel #11*)

Blue Yodel No. 12, 37, 40

Blue Yodel Number Eleven, 34, 74, 119, 125, 126, 130, 134

Brakeman's Blues, The (Yodeling The Blues Away), 13, 64, 113, 114, 115, 116*, 117, 119, 121, 122, 129, 132, 134

Carter Family And Jimmie Rodgers In Texas, The, 52, 77, 110, 119, 123, 127, 131, 134

Cow Hand's Last Ride, The, 37, 40, 74

Daddy And Home, 16, 49, 50, 78, 101, 102, 112, 113, 114*, 115, 116, 120, 121*, 127, 129, 134

Dear Old Sunny South, 101

Dear Old Sunny South By The Sea, 15, 51, 113, 116, 120, 121, 122, 125, 127, 128, 129, 131*

Desert Blues, 39, 70, 113, 118, 119, 122, 124, 128, 130, 134

Down The Old Road To Home, 30, 31, 42, 60, 81

Dreaming With Tears In My Eyes, 53, 77, 78, 111

Everybody Does It In Hawaii, 17, 118, 126, 134

For The Sake Of Days Gone By, 28, 48, 67, 105, 118, 125, 126, 130, 135

Frankie And Johnny, 17, 45, 57, 69, 72, 84, 105*, 113, 116, 118, 119, 121, 122*, 125, 131, 132

Gambling Barroom Blues, 33, 41, 55, 60, 80

Gambling Polka Dot Blues, 27, 110*, 119, 123, 124, 127, 135

High Powered Mama, 21, 104, 117, 123, 124, 127, 135

Hobo Bill's Last Ride, 19, 20, 63, 115, 117, 125, 127, 129, 131, 132

Hobo's Meditation, 30, 31, 61, 111

Home Call, 29, 66, 105*, 115, 118, 120, 125, 128, 135

If Brother Jack Were Here, 13

I'm Free (From The Chain Gang Now), 36, 71

I'm Lonely And Blue, 38, 58, 66, 104, 118, 123, 126, 129, 135

I'm Lonesome Too, 24, 48, 67, 105, 118, 123, 126, 130, 135

I'm Sorry We Met, 16, 113, 118, 119, 122, 124, 128, 135

In The Hills Of Tennessee, 32, 48, 59, 108

In The Jailhouse Now, 12, 45, 57, 72, 84, 118, 121, 122, 126, 129, 135

In The Jail-House Now – No. 2, 21, 69, 73, 101, 112, 115, 117, 121, 123, 128, 130, 131, 132

I've Only Loved Three Women, 52, 77

I've Ranged, I've Roamed, I've Travelled, 49, 76, 107*, 119, 122, 124, 126, 136

Jimmie Rodger's Last Blue Yodel, 45, 58, 69, 84

Jimmie Rodger's Last Ride, 45

Jimmie Rodger's Medley Part 1, 101

Jimmie Rodger's Medley Part 2, 101

Jimmie Rodger's Puzzle Record, 109 (see also *Rodger's Puzzle Record*)

Jimmie Rodgers Visits The Carter Family, 25, 72, 109, 119, 122, 123, 127, 131

Jimmie The Kid (Parts Of The Life Of Rodgers), 23, 24, 75, 76, 109, 118, 122, 125, 128, 130, 131, 136

Jimmie's Mean Mama Blues, 22, 73, 113, 114, 116, 120, 127, 130

Jimmie's Texas Blues, 19, 64, 117, 124, 127, 132, 136

Land Of My Boyhood Dreams, The, 35, 46, 70, 74, 84, 106*, 119, 123, 125, 126, 136

Let Me Be Your Side Track, 26, 27, 43, 63, 82, 109*, 117, 125, 127

Long Tall Mamma Blues, 33, 60

145

Looking For A New Mama, 25, 41, 55, 60, 79, 80, 110, 118, 125, 128

Lullaby Yodel, 15, 16, 45, 46, 66, 84, 117, 124, 127, 128, 129, 131*, 136

Memphis Yodel, 15, 16, 70, 73, 103, 136

Miss The Mississippi And You, 32, 42, 62, 81, 115, 120

Mississippi Delta Blues, 35

Mississippi Moon, 29, 30, 44, 56, 57, 67, 83, 103*, 117, 136

Mississippi River Blues, 23, 46, 72, 107, 118, 124, 125, 126, 130, 132, 136

Moonlight And Skies, 24, 25, 40, 54*, 65, 71, 79, 104, 118, 121, 122, 123, 126, 130, 131, 137

Mother, Queen Of My Heart, 31, 42, 56, 61, 62, 81, 102, 112, 115, 120

Mule Skinner Blues (see also *Blue Yodel No. 8 & Muleskinner Blues*), 51

Muleskinner Blues (see also *Mule Skinner Blues & Blue Yodel No. 8)*, 101

My Blue Eyed Jane, 23, 24, 46, 68, 104, 117, 122, 128, 130, 132, 137

My Carolina Sunshine Girl, 39, 46, 47, 70, 113, 114, 115, 116, 117, 120, 121, 122, 125, 129, 132*, 137

My Good Gal's Gone – Blues, 49, 76, 110, 117, 123, 125, 127

My Little Lady, 38, 39, 49, 75, 76, 114, 116, 120, 127, 129, 131, 137

My Little Old Home Down In New Orleans, 15, 47, 66, 117, 122, 124, 127, 129, 137

My Mother Was A Lady, 13, 14, 46, 68, 119, 126, 129

My Old Pal, 16, 47, 78, 101, 113, 118, 119, 121, 122, 124, 128, 129, 137

My Rough And Rowdy Ways, 17, 18, 65, 106, 107, 117, 121, 122, 128, 132, 137

My Time Ain't Long, 28, 29, 43, 56, 82, 111*

Mystery Of Number Five, The, 22, 48, 68, 119, 121, 125, 126, 130

Never No Mo' Blues, 14, 50, 102, 112*, 113, 114*, 115, 116, 120, 121, 127, 128, 129, 131, 137

Ninety Nine Years Blues, 28, 29, 65

No Hard Times, 32, 33, 61, 108

Nobody Knows But Me, 22, 73, 119, 126, 130, 138

Old Pal Of My Heart, 35, 44, 57, 83, 114

Old Love Letters (Bring Memories Of You), 36, 37, 50, 71

One Rose, The (That's Left In My Heart), 52, 117, 128, 129, 130, 131, 132*

Peach Pickin' Time Down In Georgia (see also *Peach Picking Time In Georgia*), 33, 34, 42, 56, 59, 81, 112, 115

Peach Picking Time In Georgia (see also *Peach Pickin' Time Down In Georgia*), 102, 115, 120

Pistol Packin' Papa, 21, 69, 75, 113, 116, 120, 121, 125, 127, 130, 138

Prairie Lullaby, 33, 34, 41, 42, 55, 56, 60, 80, 114

Prohibition Has Done Me Wrong, 108

Pullman Porters, The, 103

Rock All Our Babies To Sleep, 31, 40, 54*, 59, 79

Rodgers' Puzzle Record (see also *Jimmie Rodger's Puzzle Record*), 26, 27, 109

Roll Along Kentucky Moon, 28, 43, 66, 82, 111

Round Up Time Out West When The Cactus Is In Bloom, 27

Sailor's Plea, The 38, 51, 53, 76, 103, 118, 123, 126, 129, 138

She Was Happy Till She Met You, 29, 41, 55, 62, 69, 80, 107, 118, 126, 130, 138

She's More To Be Pitied Than Censured, 69

Singing Brakeman, The, 101

Sleep, Baby, Sleep, 11, 50, 71, 113, 118, 120, 124, 128*, 129, 131*

Soldier's Sweetheart, The, 11, 53, 71, 118, 122, 125, 126, 129, 138

Somewhere Down Below The Dixon Line, 36, 71

Southern Cannon-Ball, 35, 74, 110, 117, 123, 125, 128, 131, 132, 138

Sweet Mama Hurry Home Or I'll Be Gone, 34, 74

T For Texas (see *Blue Yodel #1 T For Texas*)

T.B. Blues, 23, 51, 59, 75, 108, 118, 126, 130

Take Me Back Again, 53, 104, 118, 123, 126, 130, 138

That's Why I'm Blue, 20, 50, 67, 68, 119, 121, 126, 138

Those Gambler's Blues, 21, 63, 105, 119, 123, 126, 130

Train Whistle Blues, 19, 68, 115, 117, 124, 127, 132, 139

Travellin' Blues, 24, 75, 108*, 115, 117, 120, 125, 128, 130, 132, 139

Treasures Untold, 13, 14, 48, 65, 66, 115, 117, 121, 124, 127, 128, 129, 131, 139

Tuck Away My Lonesome Blues, 17, 18, 47, 76, 113, 118, 120, 124, 128, 139

Waiting For A Train, 37, 44, 57, 78, 83, 113, 114*, 116, 120, 121*, 127, 129, 131, 132, 139

What's It?, 26, 43, 62, 82, 110, 119, 123, 127, 139

When The Cactus Is In Bloom, 27, 44, 57, 65, 83, 110, 118, 125, 126, 132

Whippin' That Old T.B., 32, 33, 41, 42, 55, 56, 61, 80, 108

Whisper Your Mother's Name, 18, 19, 41, 55, 62, 80, 105, 106, 123, 125, 139

Why Did You Give Me Your Love, 49, 76, 107, 119, 121, 123, 125, 126, 130, 139

Why Should I Be Lonely, 26, 42, 61, 81, 82, 118, 121, 126, 130, 132, 140

Why There's A Tear In My Eye, 51, 77, 109, 119, 125, 126, 130, 131

Wonderful City, The, 52, 77, 119, 125, 126, 131, 140

Years Ago, 45, 58, 70, 84

Yodeling Cowboy, 18, 50, 59, 64, 118, 126, 140

Yodeling My Way Back Home, 52, 77, 78

Yodeling Ranger, The, 36, 47, 71

You And My Old Guitar, 38, 39, 43, 56, 68, 82, 114, 115, 116, 120, 125, 127, 129, 140

Made in the USA
Las Vegas, NV
19 February 2024